Fresh Ways with
Pasta

COVER
In a spaghetti appetizer, lightly sautéed strips of courgette and carrot coil like the pasta itself (recipe, page 48). Red onion and garlic compound the dish's flavour without adding a heavy load of calories.

TIME-LIFE BOOKS

EUROPEAN EDITOR: Ellen Phillips
Design Director: Ed Skyner
Director of Editorial Resources: Samantha Hill
Chief Sub-Editor: Ilse Gray

Correspondents: Elisabeth Kraemer-Singh (Bonn); Dorothy Bacon (London); Maria Vincenza Aloisi, Josephine du Brusle (Paris); Ann Natanson (Rome).

LOST CIVILIZATIONS
HOW THINGS WORK
SYSTEM EARTH
LIBRARY OF CURIOUS AND UNUSUAL FACTS
BUILDING BLOCKS
A CHILD'S FIRST LIBRARY OF LEARNING
VOYAGE THROUGH THE UNIVERSE
THE THIRD REICH
MYSTERIES OF THE UNKNOWN
TIME-LIFE HISTORY OF THE WORLD
FITNESS, HEALTH AND NUTRITION
HEALTHY HOME COOKING
UNDERSTANDING COMPUTERS
THE ENCHANTED WORLD
LIBRARY OF NATIONS
PLANET EARTH
THE GOOD COOK
THE WORLD'S WILD PLACES

New edition © 1995 Time-Life Books Inc. All rights reserved.
This edition published 1995 by Brockhampton Press, a member of Hodder Headline PLC.
First published 1986 by Time-Life Books Inc.

ISBN 1 86019 056 1
TIME-LIFE is a trademark of Time Warner Inc. U.S.A.

HEALTHY HOME COOKING

SERIES DIRECTOR: Dale M. Brown
Deputy Editor: Barbara Fleming
Series Administrator: Elise Ritter Gibson
Designer: Herbert H. Quarmby
Picture Editor: Sally Collins
Photographer: Renée Comet
Text Editor: Allan Fallow
Editorial Assistant: Rebecca C. Christofferson

Editorial Staff for *Fresh Ways with Pasta:*
Book Manager: Barbara Sause
Assistant Picture Editor: Scarlet Cheng
Writer: Margery A. duMond
Researcher/Writer: Jean Getlin
Copy Co-ordinators: Marfé Ferguson, Elizabeth Graham,
Picture Co-ordinator: Linda Yates
Photographer's Assistant: Rina M. Ganassa

European Edition:
Designer: Lynne Brown
Sub-Editor: Wendy Gibbons
Production Co-ordinator: Nikki Allen
Production Assistant: Maureen Kelly

THE COOKS

ADAM DE VITO began his cooking apprenticeship when he was only 14. He has worked at Le Pavillon restaurant, in Washington, D.C., taught with cookery author Madeleine Kamman, and conducted classes at L'Académie de Cuisine in Maryland.

HENRY GROSSI was awarded a Grand Diplôme at the École de Cuisine La Varenne in Paris. He then served as the school's assistant director and as its North American business and publications co-ordinator.

JOHN T. SHAFFER is a graduate of The Culinary Institute of America at Hyde Park, New York. He has had a broad experience as a chef, including five years at The Four Seasons Hotel in Washington, D.C.

CONSULTANTS

CAROL CUTLER is the author of many cookery books. During the 12 years she lived in France, she studied at the Cordon Bleu and the École des Trois Gourmandes, as well as with private chefs. She is a member of the Cercle des Gourmettes and a charter member and past president of Les Dames d'Escoffier.

NORMA MACMILLAN has written several cookery books and edited many others. She has worked on various cookery publications, including *Grand Diplôme* and *Supercook.* She lives and works in London.

PAT ALBUREY is a home economist with a wide experience of preparing foods for photography, teaching cookery and creating recipes. She has been involved in a number of cookery books and was the studio consultant for the Time-Life series *The Good Cook.*

SHARON FARRINGTON, a food writer and consultant specializing in Asian cuisines, developed most of the recipes for the Asian-pasta section of this book. Raised in Oregon, she learnt how to prepare Asian food while living in Thailand.

NUTRITION CONSULTANTS

JANET TENNEY has been involved in nutrition and consumer affairs since she received her master's degree in human nutrition from Columbia University. She is the manager for developing and implementing nutritional programmes for a major chain of supermarkets.

PATRICIA JUDD trained as a dietician and worked in hospital practice before returning to university to obtain her MSc and PhD degrees. For the last 10 years she has lectured in Nutrition and Dietetics at London University.

This volume is one of a series of illustrated cookery books that emphasizes the preparation of healthy dishes for today's weight-conscious, nutrition-minded eaters.

Fresh Ways with Pasta

BY

THE EDITORS OF TIME-LIFE BOOKS

Contents

Tomato Fettuccine with Artichokes and Mint

Pasta Shells and Scallops

Crab Pillows

Egg Noodles with Poppy Seeds, Yogurt and Mushrooms

3 The World of Asian Noodles 101

Spaghetti with Fresh Basil, Pine-Nuts and Cheese

Duckling Dumplings and Ginger-Plum Sauce

Japanese Summer Noodles with Prawns

4 Pasta in the Microwave Oven 131

Bravo, Pasta!

Pasta is easy, and pasta is cheap. Better yet, it is good for you. It has become the preferred food of many sportsmen and women before a race or match, packing its own wallop of energy. And weight-conscious cooks can delight in the knowledge that pasta is not the fattening food everyone thought it was.

What makes pasta exceptional? Its wheat-flour starch, for one thing. A complex carbohydrate, the starch provides as much energy as pure protein. Moreover, pasta is easy to digest, and it provides a long-lasting feeling of satisfaction that can be a boon to girth-watchers by curtailing their appetites. The wonder is that a food so sustaining should have relatively few calories: 150 g (5 oz) of cooked spaghetti contains a slender 200 calories, less than half those in the equivalent weight of sirloin steak.

Pasta has further advantages. Its protein is made up of six of the eight essential amino acids; for pasta to be a complete food, all it needs is a little meat or grated cheese to round out and enhance its protein. Pasta also contains niacin, thiamine and riboflavin, calcium and iron, and fibre. Sauced wisely and well, a pasta dish served with a fresh green salad, and followed by a fruit dessert, is a perfect meal, high in satisfaction and nutrition.

Pasta's infinite variety

Pasta is traditionally defined as a wheat-paste food made from flour and water. This book stretches that definition to include Asian noodles, which can be made from rice, mung beans, buckwheat or other ingredients, as well as wheat. The dried commercial variety is generally produced from protein-rich semolina, the coarsely ground endosperm of kernels of hard durum wheat. When water is added to semolina flour and the dough is worked, gluten is developed and a resilient dough is formed. The dough is then extruded or stamped out under great pressure by machine, and the resulting pasta is carefully dried. Occasionally eggs are added to yield the egg noodles so popular in Central European dishes. Most dried pasta has a long shelf life and can be safely stored in a dry place for up to two years without losing flavour.

While dried pasta is best when made with semolina, fresh pasta can be prepared at home with ordinary flour. In this book the fresh pasta recipes call for unbleached strong plain flour, or finely milled semolina combined with the strong plain flour. Fortunately, finely milled semolina is becoming increasingly available in supermarkets (the coarsely milled type absorbs water poorly and is difficult to work with by hand). The recipes tell how much water to add to the dough — but since flours differ in their ability to absorb moisture, more may be used if the dough proves too stiff to roll out easily by hand or through a pasta machine.

The four sections that follow sing the praises of pasta. Though they concentrate on pasta as a main course, they also present recipes for pasta appetizers and side dishes. The first section deals with fresh pasta and shows, in a series of step-by-step photographs, how to make and shape pasta and how to stuff several kinds with savoury fillings. The second section concentrates on dried pasta, including egg noodles. The third delves into Asian noodles and dumplings, and it too utilizes photographs to demonstrate methods of making and shaping them. The fourth section puts the microwave oven to work cooking a variety of pasta dishes.

Since pasta comes in a dizzying range of sizes and shapes, pages 44-45 and 102-103 illustrate all the types called for in the recipes and identify them by the names under which you are likely to find them in the shops. But the varying names of the shapes of pasta, particularly those from Italy, can be confusing. Names commonly used in northern Italy, for instance, often differ from those in the south, so when buying pasta it is best to look for the shape rather than the name.

In buying dried pasta, examine the label to be certain that the pasta has been produced with semolina. Pastas made with all or part farina, the coarsely ground endosperm of any wheat except durum, should be avoided because they turn pasty during the boiling. When cooked, good pasta can swell to nearly three times its size and possesses a slightly nutty, sweet flavour.

As for cooking, two rules apply: use a lot of boiling water and be sure not to overcook the pasta *(box, page 9)*. While almost all the recipes in this book call for salting the water, the quantity used is less than that required by many other cookery books. Cooks should bear in mind that the salt is highly diluted when adequate water is used and that a relatively small amount of salt is absorbed by the pasta. Leave it out entirely, and the pasta will be insipid, unless coupled with an intensely flavoured sauce. Some cooks find that a little lemon juice in the water makes a fairly good substitute for salt.

The question of portion size

For consistency's sake, this book employs the same standard measure for a single serving as most pasta manufacturers recommend — 60 g (2 oz) dried for 150 g (5 oz) cooked. Most people will probably agree that with a food as popular as pasta 150 g (5 oz) constitutes rather scant eating when presented as a main course. Cooks should feel free to prepare and serve as much pasta as they want so long as they take into account the greater calories the larger portion entails and the caloric value of the rest of the meal, as well as that of the remainder of the day's eating.

The recipes for accompanying sauces list fresh ingredients for maximum flavour and nutrition, but because juicy, well-ripened tomatoes are sometimes unavailable, the recipes offer the option of using whole canned tomatoes. Whole tomatoes are preferred

The Key to Better Eating

This book, like others in the Healthy Home Cooking series, presents an analysis of nutrients contained in a single serving of each dish, listed beside the recipe itself, as on the right. Approximate counts for calories, protein, cholesterol, total fat (the kind that increases the body's blood cholesterol) and sodium are given.

Healthy Home Cooking addresses the concerns of today's weight-conscious, health-minded cooks by providing recipes that fall within guidelines set by nutritionists. The secret to eating well, of course, has to do with maintaining a balance of foods in the diet; most of us consume too much sugar and salt, too much fat and too many calories, even too much protein.

Interpreting the chart

The chart below gives dietary guidelines for healthy men, women and children. Recommended figures vary from country to country, but the principles are the same everywhere. Here, the average daily amounts of calories and protein are from a report by the U.K. Department of Health and Social Security; the maximum advisable daily intake of fat is based on guidelines given by the National Advisory Committee on Nutrition Education (NACNE); those for cholesterol and sodium are based on upper limits suggested by the World Health Organisation.

The volumes in the Healthy Home Cooking series do not purport to be diet books, nor do they focus on health foods. Rather, they express a commonsense approach to cooking that uses salt, sugar, cream, butter and oil in moderation while employing other ingredients that also provide flavour and satisfaction. Herbs, spices, aromatic vegetables, fruits and peels, and juices, wines and vinegars are all used towards this end.

The recipes make few unusual demands. Naturally they call for fresh ingredients, offering substitutes when these are unavailable. (The substitute is not calculated in the nutrient analysis, however.) Most of the

---

Calories **285**
Protein **11g**
Cholesterol **5mg**
Total fat **6g**
Saturated fat **2g**
Sodium **350mg**

---

pastas and sauce ingredients can be found in any well-stocked supermarket; exceptions can be bought in speciality or ethnic shops.

In planning a meal, the cook using the recipes should consider what the rest of the meal is likely to contribute nutritionally. The cook should also bear in mind that moderate portions are always recommended.

In Healthy Home Cooking's test kitchens, heavy-bottomed pots and pans are used to guard against burning the food whenever a small amount of oil is used and where there is danger of the food adhering to the hot surface, but non-stick pans can be utilized as well. Both safflower oil and virgin olive oil are favoured for sautéing. Safflower was chosen because it is the most highly polyunsaturated vegetable fat available in supermarkets, and polyunsaturated fats reduce blood cholesterol; if unobtainable, use sunflower oil, also

high in polyunsaturated fats. Virgin olive oil is used because it has a fine fruity flavour lacking in the lesser grade known as "pure". In addition, it is — like all olive oil — high in monounsaturated fats, which are thought not to increase blood cholesterol. Sometimes the two oils are combined, with the olive oil contributing its fruitiness to the safflower oil. When virgin olive oil is unavailable, "pure" may be substituted.

About cooking times

To help the cook plan ahead, Healthy Home Cooking takes time into account in its recipes. While recognizing that everyone cooks at a different speed, and that stoves and ovens differ, the series provides approximate "working" and "total" times for every dish. Working time stands for the actual minutes spent on preparation; total time includes unattended cooking time, as well as time devoted to marinating, steeping or soaking. Since the recipes emphasize fresh foods, they may take a bit longer to prepare than dishes that call for canned or packaged products, but the payoff in flavour and often in nutrition should compensate for the little extra time involved.

Recommended Dietary Guidelines

		Average Daily Intake		Maximum Daily Intake			
		CALORIES	PROTEIN grams	CHOLESTEROL milligrams	TOTAL FAT grams	SATURATED FAT grams	SODIUM milligrams
Females	7-8	1900	47	300	80	32	2000*
	9-11	2050	51	300	77	35	2000
	12-17	2150	53	300	81	36	2000
	18-54	2150	54	300	81	36	2000
	54-74	1900	47	300	72	32	2000
Males	7-8	1980	49	300	80	33	2000
	9-11	2280	57	300	77	38	2000
	12-14	2640	66	300	99	44	2000
	15-17	2880	72	300	108	48	2000
	18-34	2900	72	300	109	48	2000
	35-64	2750	69	300	104	35	2000
	65-74	2400	60	300	91	40	2000

*(or 5g salt)

to canned puréed or chopped tomatoes as having better flavour; after draining, they can be easily puréed or chopped. A well-made tomato sauce is one of dining's great pleasures, and it should not be degraded by being dusted with inferior pre-grated Parmesan. Freshly grated cheese is in order.

Now that pasta is no longer being maligned as a fattening food, it may be enjoyed to the full. But people should guard against raising the calorie count of a dish by going overboard on the sauce — as is all too often the case — or the bread.

Those pasta lovers, the Italians, know how to sauce a pasta well, which means lightly, and since they often consume it as a first course, they see no need for bread. And they know how to eat pasta properly too — with all the relish that this wonderfully varied, yet amazingly simple, food inspires.

How to Cook Pasta

Pasta is easy to cook; yet all too often it emerges soggy and sticky. Only a few steps need to be followed to ensure perfectly cooked pasta every time.

☐ Use a big pan and lots of water. As the often repeated expression has it, pasta loves to swim.

☐ Let the water come to a full boil, then add the salt.

☐ With the water at a full boil, drop in the pasta, a few handfuls at a time; stir it to keep it from sticking.

☐ Cover the pan so the water can come back to the boil quickly. Then uncover the pot to prevent boiling over, and adjust the heat to maintain a rolling boil.

☐ Begin timing the pasta once the water has resumed boiling. Test for doneness by biting into a piece of the pasta; when the pasta is *al dente* — that is, just right to the tooth, deliciously chewy without a floury taste — it is ready. Logic dictates that pastas of different thicknesses will take varying times to cook and that fresh pasta, with its higher moisture content, will cook faster than dried. How long a box of pasta has been on the grocer's shelf or on your own can matter too; the older the pasta, the drier it is likely to be and the longer therefore the cooking time. Manufacturers' instructions are not always reliable; the tooth test is safer.

☐ Drain the pasta at once. Do not rinse it unless the recipe says so (rinsing washes away nutrients).

☐ Sauce the pasta at once to keep it from sticking to itself and toss it well to distribute the sauce.

EDITOR'S NOTE: *All recipes for dried and fresh pastas in this book include recommended testing or cooking times. In most of the recipes, pasta is cooked according to the following proportions of water and salt:*

PASTA	WATER	SALT
125-175 g (4-6 oz)	2 litres (3½ pints)	1 tsp
250-300 g (8-10 oz)	3 litres (5 pints)	1½ tsp
350-500 g (12-16 oz)	4 litres (7 pints)	2 tsp

1 *Nests of home-made pasta demonstrate the variety achieved when ingredients as diverse as cocoa, carrots, beetroots, tomato and spinach are added to dough.*

The Fun of Making Your Own

One of the pleasures of fresh pasta is making it yourself. You can experiment with a variety of shapes — perhaps even inventing your own — and you can add different flavours and colourful vegetable purées to the dough to please both palate and eye. Photographs on the following pages will show you how.

This section examines fresh pasta's many possibilities — as a starter, main course or side dish. The accompanying sauces, although created to go with a particular pasta, could as easily complement another fresh pasta or a dried pasta of a corresponding shape.

The difference between fresh and dried pasta lies not just in the freshness of the product but in the kinds of flour used. Most dried pastas are held together by the high gluten content of the semolina dough with which they are made. In this section pasta is prepared with unbleached strong plain flour and eggs or with a mixture of finely milled semolina and unbleached strong plain flour. One recipe also includes buckwheat flour, which, despite its name, contains no wheat at all; it consists instead of the ground seeds of the flowering buckwheat plant.

Recipes for fresh pasta doughs usually call for two eggs with 175 g (6 oz) of flour. In this section, to keep down the cholesterol in the dough, an egg white is substituted for one of the whole eggs. The recipes using semolina have no eggs at all.

Home-made pasta can be refrigerated for 24 hours when covered with plastic film, or the pasta can be frozen. It is rarely so good, however, as when it is eaten soon after being made. Since it has a relatively high moisture content, it need not be cooked long. And this has the advantage of allowing the ingredients with which some of the doughs have been coloured — from spinach and tomatoes to carrots, beetroot and curry — to shine through undiminished.

Using a Pasta Machine

Making fresh pasta is greatly simplified when a good pasta machine takes over the job that otherwise would have to be done entirely by hand. You can quickly turn out noodles, or sheets of dough that may be cut and twisted into fancy shapes, such as bow ties, or used for ravioli and tortellini. Photographs on these two pages demonstrate the preparation of the basic dough.

The trick is to roll out the dough repeatedly: it should have a sheen and be satiny to the touch when ready. If the dough gets sticky, flour it well on both sides before running it through again.

You can cook the pasta immediately, or you can reserve all or part of it for later use. To dry it, hang the strands over a pasta drying rack or twist the strands loosely into "nests" on a lightly floured surface. When the pasta is thoroughly dry, store it in airtight containers.

To freeze fresh pasta, let it dry for 15 minutes or so. Then coil handfuls into nests of serving portion size and place these on a tray. Put the tray in the freezer for an hour; the stiffened pasta can then be stored in heavy-duty polythene bags in the freezer. To cook frozen pasta, put it directly into boiling water, without thawing.

1 *ADDING EGG AND OIL TO FLOUR. Place 175 g (6 oz) flour in a mixing bowl and make a well in the centre. Drop one whole egg and one egg white into the well, then add 1 tablespoon of oil. (Alternatively, the dough can be prepared in a food processor following directions for basic pasta dough on page 15.)*

2 *BLENDING THE INGREDIENTS. With a wooden spoon or a fork, break the yolk and mix it together with the whites and oil. Then broaden your strokes to incorporate the flour, and continue to mix until all the liquid is absorbed and the dough can be gathered into a ball, adding more flour if necessary.*

3 *KNEADING BY HAND. Divide the dough into thirds. Cover two of the pieces with plastic film or a bowl to keep them from drying out. On a lightly floured work surface — preferably wood or marble — knead the third piece for several minutes. If the dough feels tough and inelastic, cover it and let it rest for 15 minutes.*

4 KNEADING BY MACHINE. *Flatten the dough to about 2.5 cm (1 inch) thickness and lightly flour both sides. Adjust the pasta machine's smooth rollers for the widest setting. Pass the dough through the feeder, cranking the rollers with one hand and catching the dough with the other as it is extruded.*

5 FOLDING THE ROLLED DOUGH. *On a lightly floured surface, fold the piece into thirds and press it down to flatten it; then run it lengthwise through the machine once more. Repeat the process six to eight times, folding the dough into thirds each time. In the end, the surface should be smooth and satiny.*

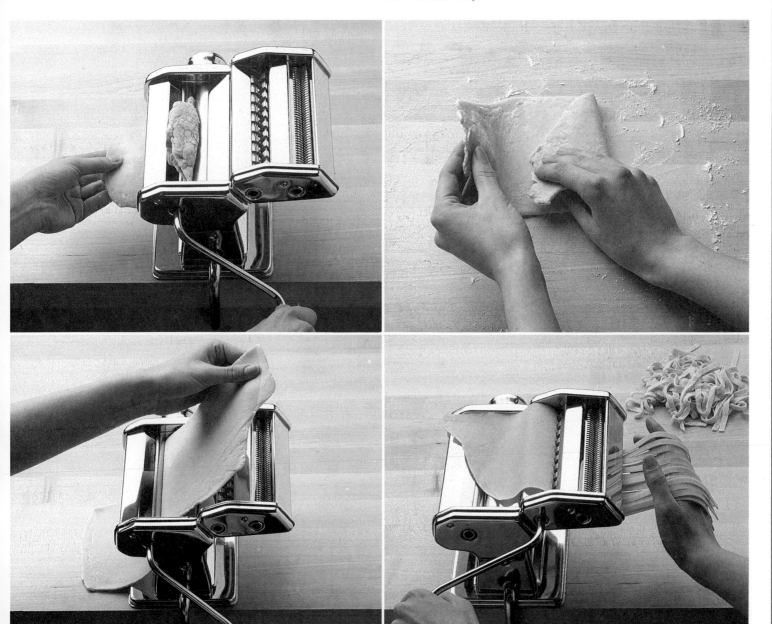

6 REDUCING THE THICKNESS. *Adjust the control to the next smaller setting, and feed the entire sheet through the machine, without folding. Repeat the procedure, narrowing the setting each time, until the desired thickness is achieved — usually with the next-to-last setting. Flour the dough as necessary to prevent sticking, and support the sheet with your free hand to keep it as extended and flat as possible going into and coming out of the rollers.*

7 CUTTING NOODLES. *With a knife, cut the sheet of dough in half for easier manageability. Flour the strips lightly on both sides and allow them to rest for 10 to 15 minutes before handling them again. Then run one piece of dough at a time through the selected cutting rollers. Gently toss the noodles in flour and set them aside before cutting the next sheet. Repeat the procedures with the remaining sheets of dough.*

Mushroom-Stuffed Triangles

Serves 6 as an appetizer
Working (and total) time: about 50 minutes

Calories **265**
Protein **10g**
Cholesterol **60mg**
Total fat **8g**
Saturated fat **3g**
Sodium **290mg**

	basic or semolina pasta dough (opposite)	
15 g	dried wild mushrooms, preferably ceps, soaked for 20 minutes in enough boiling water to cover them	½ oz
250 g	fresh mushrooms, wiped clean and finely chopped	8 oz
2	large shallots, finely chopped	2
3	garlic cloves, finely chopped	3
2 tbsp	balsamic vinegar, or 1 tbsp red wine vinegar	2 tbsp
4 tbsp	red wine	4 tbsp
¼ tsp	salt	¼ tsp
	freshly ground black pepper	
2 tbsp	fresh breadcrumbs	2 tbsp
1.25 kg	ripe tomatoes, skinned, seeded and chopped, or 800 g (28 oz) canned whole tomatoes, drained and chopped	2½ lb
1	large onion, chopped	1
3	carrots (about 250 g/8 oz), peeled and chopped	3
3 tbsp	double cream	3 tbsp
40 g	Parmesan cheese, freshly grated	1½ oz

To make the filling, drain the wild mushrooms, reserving their liquid. Finely chop them and transfer them to a large, heavy frying pan. Add the fresh mushrooms, shallots and two thirds of the garlic. Pour in the reserved mushroom-soaking liquid and bring the liquid to the boil over medium-high heat. Cook the mixture until nearly all the liquid has evaporated — about 5 minutes. Add the vinegar, wine, half of the salt and a generous grinding of pepper. Continue cooking, stirring constantly, until all the liquid has boiled away — about 3 minutes more. Stir in the breadcrumbs and set the mixture aside to cool.

To make the sauce, combine the tomatoes, onion, carrots, some pepper, the remaining garlic and the remaining salt in a saucepan. Add 4 tablespoons of water and bring the liquid to the boil. Cook the mixture until the vegetables are soft and very little of the liquid remains —about 20 minutes. Purée the sauce in a food processor or blender and return it to

the saucepan. Stir in the cream and set the pan aside.

Meanwhile, prepare the triangles. First divide the pasta dough into four portions. Cover three of the portions with plastic film or an inverted bowl to keep them from drying out. Roll out the fourth portion to form a long strip about 12.5 cm (5 inches) wide and about 1 mm (1/16 inch) thick *(pages 12-13)*. Cut across the dough at 12.5 cm (5 inch) intervals to form squares, then cut each of the squares into four smaller ones.

Mound about 1 teaspoon of the filling in the centre of a square. Moisten the edges of two adjacent sides of the square. Fold the moistened edges over the filling to form a triangle, and press the edges closed. Repeat the process with the remaining dough and filling.

Add the filled pasta triangles to 3 litres (5 pints) of boiling water with 1½ teaspoons of salt. Start testing the triangles after 1 minute and cook them until they are *al dente*.

Reheat the sauce over medium-high heat; if the sauce is too thick to pour easily, add 1 to 2 tablespoons of the pasta-cooking water. Drain the triangles and transfer them to a serving dish, then pour the warmed sauce over them. Serve immediately; pass the Parmesan cheese separately.

Basic Pasta Dough

Serves 4

Calories **205**
Protein **7g**
Cholesterol **60mg**
Total fat **7g**
Saturated fat **1g**
Sodium **30mg**

175 to 200 g	strong plain flour	6 to 7 oz
1	egg	1
1	egg white	1
1 tbsp	safflower oil	1 tbsp

To prepare the dough in a food processor, put 175 g (6 oz) of the flour, the egg, egg white and oil in the bowl of the machine and process the mixture for about 30 seconds. If the mixture forms a ball immediately and is wet to the touch, mix in flour by the tablespoon until the dough feels soft but not sticky. If the mixture does not form a ball, try pinching it together with your fingers. If it is still too dry to work with, blend in water by the teaspoon until the dough just forms a ball. If you have a pasta machine, the dough may be immediately kneaded and rolled out *(pages 12-13)*.

To prepare the dough by hand, put 175 g (6 oz) of the flour into a mixing bowl and make a well in the centre. Add the egg, egg white and oil to the well and stir them with a fork or wooden spoon, gradually mixing in the flour. Transfer the dough to a lightly floured surface and

knead it for a few minutes. The dough should come cleanly away from the surface; if it is too wet, add flour by the tablespoon until the dough is no longer sticky. If the dough is too dry and crumbly to work with, add water by the teaspoon until it is pliable. Continue kneading the dough until it is smooth and elastic — about 10 minutes; alternatively, knead the dough in a pasta machine *(pages 12-13)*.

If you are not using a pasta machine, wrap the dough in greaseproof paper or plastic film and let it rest for 15 minutes before rolling it out.

EDITOR'S NOTE: *In a traditional pasta dough, two eggs are used with 175 g (6 oz) of flour. Here, to reduce the amount of cholesterol in the dough, an egg white has been substituted for one of the whole eggs.*

Semolina Pasta Dough

Serves 4

Calories **230**
Protein **7g**
Cholesterol **0mg**
Total fat **1g**
Saturated fat **0g**
Sodium **5mg**

125 g	strong plain flour	4 oz
150 g	fine semolina	5 oz

To prepare the dough in a food processor, first blend the flour and semolina together, then gradually mix in up to 15 cl (¼ pint) of water until the mixture just forms a ball. If the mixture is wet to the touch, blend in flour by the tablespoon until the dough feels soft but not sticky. If the mixture does not form a ball, try pinching it together with your fingers. If it is still too dry to work with, blend in water by the teaspoon until the dough just forms a ball. If you have a pasta machine, the dough may be immediately kneaded and rolled out *(pages 12-13)*.

To prepare the dough by hand, blend the flour and semolina in a bowl and make a well in the centre. With a fork or a wooden spoon, gradually mix in up to 15 cl (¼ pint) of water until the dough can be pressed together into a solid ball. Transfer the dough to a lightly floured surface and knead it for a few minutes. The dough should come cleanly away from the surface; if it is too wet, incorporate flour a tablespoon at a time until the dough is no longer sticky. If the dough feels dry and crumbly, incorporate water by the teaspoon until it is pliable. Continue kneading until the dough is smooth and elastic — about 10 minutes; alternatively, knead the dough in a pasta machine *(pages 12-13)*.

If you are not using a pasta machine, wrap the dough in greaseproof paper or plastic film and let it rest for 15 minutes before rolling it out.

Fettuccine with Swordfish and Roasted Red Pepper

Serves 4
Working (and total) time: about 1 hour

Calories **375**	basic pasta dough (page 15)	
Protein **24g**	350 g swordfish or fresh tuna steak, trimmed	12 oz
Cholesterol **100mg**	and cut into 1 cm (½ inch) cubes	
Total fat **15g**	2 garlic cloves, finely chopped	2
Saturated fat **2g**	1 tbsp fresh lemon juice	1 tbsp
Sodium **215mg**	2 tbsp virgin olive oil	2 tbsp
	1 sweet red pepper	1
	2 tbsp chopped parsley	2 tbsp

In an ovenproof baking dish, combine the swordfish cubes, garlic, lemon juice and 1 tablespoon of the oil. Toss well, cover, and let the mixture marinate in the refrigerator for at least 30 minutes.

Roll out the dough and cut it into fettuccine *(pages 12-13)*. Set the pasta aside while you prepare the fish and red pepper.

Grill the red pepper under a preheated grill, about 5 cm (2 inches) below the heat source, turning the pepper from time to time until it is charred on all sides. Transfer the pepper to a bowl and cover the bowl with plastic film, or put the pepper in a paper bag and fold it shut; the trapped steam will loosen the skin. Peel, seed and derib the pepper, holding it over the bowl to catch any juice. Cut it into thin strips and strain the juice to remove any seeds. Set the strips and juice aside.

Preheat the oven to 200°C (400°F or Mark 6). Bake the swordfish cubes in their marinade until they are cooked through — 6 to 8 minutes.

Meanwhile, add the fettuccine to 3 litres (5 pints) of boiling water with 1½ teaspoons of salt. Start testing

the pasta after 1 minute and cook it until it is *al dente*. Drain the pasta and transfer it to a large bowl. Add the remaining tablespoon of oil, the red pepper and juice, and the parsley; toss well. Add the swordfish and its cooking liquid, toss gently, and serve at once.

Tagliarini with Prawns and Scallops

Serves 8
Working (and total) time: about 45 minutes

Calories **380**	basic pasta dough (page 15)	
Protein **23g**	spinach pasta dough (page 29)	
Cholesterol **155mg**	500 g shelled scallops	1 lb
Total fat **12g**	30 g unsalted butter	1 oz
Saturated fat **3g**	3 tbsp finely chopped shallot	3 tbsp
Sodium **480mg**	500 g Mediterranean prawns, shelled and	1 lb
	deveined, the shells reserved	
	¼ litre dry vermouth	8 fl oz
	1 small bay leaf	1
	2 tbsp safflower oil	2 tbsp
	2 tbsp cut fresh chives	2 tbsp
	¼ tsp salt	¼ tsp
	white pepper	

Roll out the pasta doughs and cut them into tagliarini — very thin noodles *(pages 12-13)*. Set the tagliarini aside while you prepare the prawn and scallop sauce.

Pull off and reserve the firm, small muscle, if there is one, from the side of each scallop. Rinse the scallops, pat them dry, and set them aside. Melt the butter in a heavy-bottomed saucepan over medium heat. Stir in the shallots and cook them until they are translucent — about 2 minutes. Add the reserved prawn shells and any reserved side muscles from the scallops; cook, stirring, for 1 minute. Pour in the vermouth and simmer the mixture for 1 minute more.

Add the bay leaf and 35 cl (12 fl oz) of water to the saucepan. Bring the liquid to the boil. Reduce the heat and simmer the liquid until it is reduced by about half — 10 to 12 minutes. Set the pan aside.

To prepare the seafood, heat the oil in a large, deep, heavy frying pan over medium-high heat. Add the prawns and scallops, and sauté them for 1½ to 2 minutes, turning the pieces frequently with a spoon. Push the seafood to one side of the pan and strain the liquid from the saucepan into the frying pan. Set the frying pan aside.

Add the tagliarini to 6 litres (10 pints) of boiling water with 3 teaspoons of salt. Start testing the tagliarini after 1 minute and cook it until it is *al dente*. Drain the pasta and add it to the frying pan with the seafood. Season with the chives, salt and some pepper, and toss gently to distribute the prawns and scallops through the pasta. Cover the pan and place it over medium heat to warm the mixture thoroughly — about 1 minute. Serve the tagliarini at once.

Parsley-Stuffed Mini-Ravioli

Serves 6
Working (and total) time: about 1 hour

Calories **215**
Protein **12g**
Cholesterol **10mg**
Total fat **4g**
Saturated fat **2g**
Sodium **330mg**

	semolina pasta dough (page 15)	
125 g	low-fat ricotta cheese	4 oz
125 g	low-fat cottage cheese	4 oz
125 g	parsley leaves, finely chopped	4 oz
30 g	Parmesan cheese, freshly grated	1 oz
¼ tsp	grated nutmeg	¼ tsp
⅛ tsp	salt	⅛ tsp
	freshly ground black pepper	
12.5 cl	skimmed milk	4 fl oz

To prepare the filling, work the ricotta and cottage cheese through a sieve into a bowl. Stir in the parsley, Parmesan cheese, nutmeg, salt and some pepper. Set the mixture aside.

Roll out the dough. Then, following the steps shown below, form it into ravioli that are each about 4 cm (1½ inches) square with ½ teaspoon of filling inside. Use only about half of the filling to stuff the squares.

To make the sauce, put the remaining filling in a pan over medium-high heat and stir in the milk. Cook the sauce until it is hot but not boiling — about 5 minutes. Keep the sauce warm while you cook the ravioli.

Add the ravioli to 3 litres (5 pints) of boiling water with 1½ teaspoons of salt. Start testing the ravioli after 1 minute and cook them until they are *al dente*, then drain them. Pour the sauce over the ravioli and serve the dish immediately.

Making Ravioli

1 *ADDING THE FILLING. Spread the rolled dough sheet on a lightly floured surface. Place dollops of the filling on half of the sheet, taking care to space them evenly, about 2.5 cm (1 inch) apart.*

2 *COVERING THE FILLING. Brush the other half of the sheet lightly with water. Then fold it gently over the mounds of filling, matching the edges as closely as possible.*

3 *CUTTING THE RAVIOLI. Starting from the folded edge, use your fingers or the side of your hand to force out the air between the mounds of filling and to seal the dough. Then cut out the ravioli with a fluted pastry wheel.*

Pressed-Leaf Ravioli in Shallot Butter

Serves 6 as a side dish or first course
Working (and total) time: about 45 minutes

Calories **175**
Protein **5g**
Cholesterol **55mg**
Total fat **8g**
Saturated fat **3g**
Sodium **110mg**

	basic pasta dough or basic semolina dough (page 15)	
30 g	combined flat-leaf parsley, dill and celery leaves, stems removed	1 oz
30 g	unsalted butter	1 oz
1 tbsp	finely chopped shallot	1 tbsp
¼ tsp	salt	¼ tsp
	freshly ground black pepper	

Divide the dough into three pieces. Cover two of the pieces with plastic film or an inverted bowl to keep them from drying out, and roll out the third piece into a sheet about 1 mm (¹⁄₁₆ inch) thick *(pages 12-13)*.

Place the pasta sheet on a lightly floured surface. Distribute one third of the leaves over half of the sheet so that they are about 1 cm (½ inch) apart. Carefully flatten each leaf in place. Lightly brush the uncovered half of the sheet with water and fold it over the leaves as shown below. Press the dough down firmly to seal the leaves in, forcing out any air bubbles.

Pass the folded sheet through the pasta machine to obtain a thickness of about 1 mm (¹⁄₁₆ inch). With a large, sharp, chef's knife, cut the sheet into 5 cm (2 inch) squares. Set the squares aside and repeat the process with the remaining dough and leaves.

Melt the butter in a large, heavy frying pan over medium-high heat. Add the shallot and salt, and sauté the shallot until it turns translucent — about 2 minutes. Remove the pan from the heat.

Add the ravioli to 3 litres (5 pints) of boiling water with 1½ teaspoons of salt. Start testing the ravioli after 2 minutes and cook them until they are *al dente*. Drain the ravioli and add them to the frying pan with the shallot butter. Shake the pan gently to coat the pasta with the butter. Sprinkle on some pepper and serve hot.

EDITOR'S NOTE: *These ravioli make an excellent accompaniment to grilled lamb or veal chops. They may also be served without the shallot butter in a clear consommé.*

Cover the pan tightly; simmer the mixture, stirring once after 4 minutes, until all of the liquid is absorbed and the buckwheat groats are tender — about 6 minutes.

Meanwhile, drop the bow ties into 2 litres (3½ pints) of boiling water with 1 teaspoon of salt. Start testing the bow ties after 1 minute and cook them until they are *al dente*. Drain the bow ties and add them to the buckwheat mixture. Stir gently and serve hot.

EDITOR'S NOTE: *To intensify the flavours of the dish, prepare it a day in advance and refrigerate it. Reheat it in a shallow baking dish in a preheated 180°C (350°F or Mark 4) oven for 10 minutes, or microwave it on high for 90 seconds.*

Bow Ties with Buckwheat and Onions

Serves 4
Working (and total) time: about 45 minutes

Calories **210**
Protein **6g**
Cholesterol **15mg**
Total fat **7g**
Saturated fat **4g**
Sodium **260mg**

	semolina pasta dough (page 15, but halve ingredients)	
30 g	unsalted butter	1 oz
90 g	onion, chopped	3 oz
	freshly ground black pepper	
100 g	toasted cracked buckwheat groats (kasha)	3½ oz
1	egg white	1
¼ tsp	salt	¼ tsp
17.5 cl	unsalted chicken stock	6 fl oz

Cut the dough in half; cover one of the halves with plastic film or an inverted bowl to keep it moist. Roll out the other half into a long rectangle about 1 mm (1/16 inch) thick *(pages 12-13)*. Following the steps demonstrated on the right, cut the rectangle into strips and form the strips into bow ties. Repeat the process to fashion bow ties from the other piece of dough.

Melt the butter in a saucepan over medium heat. Add the onion and some pepper; cook for 5 minutes, stirring occasionally. Meanwhile, put the buckwheat groats in a bowl with the egg white and blend well, then add the mixture to the saucepan. Increase the heat to high and cook, stirring constantly with a fork, until the mixture is light and fluffy — 3 to 4 minutes. Add the salt and stock, then reduce the heat to low.

Shaping Bow Ties

1 CUTTING OUT THE TIES. *With a fluted pastry wheel or a knife, trim the edges of the rolled dough sheet on a flour-dusted surface. Divide the sheet down the middle. Then cut the strips into 2.5 cm (1 inch) widths.*

2 TYING THE "KNOT". *Separate the pieces. Pinch the centre of each between your thumb and forefinger to form bows, holding down the "knot" with the index finger of your other hand.*

Butternut Agnolotti

Serves 6 as a side dish or appetizer
Working time: about 30 minutes
Total time: about 1 hour and 15 minutes

Calories **335**
Protein **9g**
Cholesterol **55mg**
Total fat **12g**
Saturated fat **3g**
Sodium **325mg**

	basic pasta dough (page 15)	
1	butternut squash (about 500 g/1 lb) halved lengthwise and seeded	1
35 cl	unsalted chicken stock	12 fl oz
2 tbsp	finely cut chives	2 tbsp
45 g	walnuts, finely chopped	1½ oz
1 tbsp	finely chopped fresh sage, or 1 tsp dried sage	1 tbsp
½ tsp	salt	½ tsp
¼ tsp	white pepper	¼ tsp
30 g	unsalted butter	1 oz
2 tbsp	finely chopped shallots	2 tbsp
2 tbsp	flour	2 tbsp
4 tbsp	sweet sherry	4 tbsp
45 g	raisins	1½ oz
45 g	sultanas	1½ oz

Preheat the oven to 200°C (400°F or Mark 4). Place the squash halves, cut sides up, on a lightly oiled baking sheet; bake them until they are soft — about 1 hour. Allow the squash to cool, then scoop out the pulp and put it in a food processor or blender with 1 tablespoon of the stock. Purée the mixture and transfer it to a bowl. Stir in the chives, walnuts, sage, half the salt and half the pepper.

Divide the dough into three pieces and set two aside, covered with an inverted bowl or plastic film. Roll out the third piece to a thickness of about 1 mm (¹⁄₁₆ inch). Using a 7.5 cm (3 inch) cutter, cut it into about 12 circles. Roll out and cut the other two pieces. Place 1 teaspoon of filling near the centre of each circle. Lightly brush the edges with water, then fold in half, pressing gently on the edges to seal in the filling.

Melt the butter in a heavy-bottomed saucepan over medium heat. Add the shallots and cook until translucent — about 2 minutes. Stir in the flour and cook, stirring, for 1 minute. Whisk in the remaining stock and the sherry, and continue cooking, whisking constantly, until the sauce thickens and turns smooth — about 1 minute more. Add the raisins and sultanas, reduce the heat to low and simmer for 3 minutes. Season with the remaining salt and pepper.

Cook the agnolotti in 3 litres (5 pints) of gently boiling water with 1½ teaspoons of salt. (If necessary to avoid overcrowding, cook the pasta in several batches.) Start testing the agnolotti after 2 minutes and cook them until they are *al dente*. With a slotted spoon, transfer them to a warmed, lightly buttered platter. Spoon the sauce over the agnolotti and serve warm.

EDITOR'S NOTE: *Pumpkin can be used instead of the butternut squash in this recipe.*

Tortellini Stuffed with Veal

TORTELLINI WERE PRIZED IN THE MIDDLE AGES IN BOLOGNA,
ITALY'S CAPITAL OF FRESH PASTA COOKERY. ACCORDING
TO LEGEND, TORTELLINI WERE MODELLED AFTER THE NAVEL OF
VENUS, THE GODDESS OF LOVE.

Serves 6
Working (and total) time: about 1 hour

Calories **310**
Protein **16g**
Cholesterol **70mg**
Total fat **13g**
Saturated fat **4g**
Sodium **360mg**

	basic pasta dough (page 15)	
2 tbsp	virgin olive oil	2 tbsp
1	onion, finely chopped	1
1	carrot, peeled and finely chopped	1
1	stick celery, finely chopped	1
4	garlic cloves, very finely chopped	4
250 g	veal, minced	8 oz
¼ tsp	salt	¼ tsp
	freshly ground black pepper	
1 litre	unsalted chicken stock	1¾ pints
4 tbsp	Marsala	4 tbsp
2 tbsp	tomato paste	2 tbsp
¼ tsp	grated nutmeg	¼ tsp
4 tbsp	freshly grated Parmesan cheese	4 tbsp
2 tbsp	chopped parsley	2 tbsp

Heat the oil in a large frying pan over medium-high heat. Add the onion, carrot, celery and garlic, and cook them, stirring often, until the onion is translucent — about 4 minutes. Add the veal and continue cooking, turning the mixture frequently with a spatula or wooden spoon, until the veal is no longer pink — about 5 minutes. Add the salt and some pepper, ¼ litre (8 fl oz) of the stock, the Marsala and the tomato paste. Cover the pan, reduce the heat to medium, and cook for 30 minutes. Remove the pan from the heat and stir in the nutmeg and half of the cheese.

To prepare the pasta, roll out the dough *(pages 12-13)* and form it into tortellini *(right)*, using 1 teaspoon of the veal mixture to fill each circle. Set the tortellini aside.

To make the sauce, reduce the remaining ¾ litre (1¼ pints) of stock by one third over high heat —about 5 minutes. Stir in the parsley and keep the sauce warm.

Add the tortellini to 3 litres (5 pints) of boiling water with 1½ teaspoons of salt. Start testing the tortellini 2 to 3 minutes after the water returns to the boil and cook them until they are *al dente*. Drain the pasta and transfer it to a bowl. Pour the sauce over the tortellini and pass the remaining 2 tablespoons of Parmesan cheese separately.

Shaping the Tortellini

1 *FILLING THE TORTELLINI. With a 6 to 7.5 cm (2½ to 3 inch) pastry cutter, cut circles from the dough. Stack them or store them under a bowl to keep them from drying out. Place some filling on a circle, then moisten half the edge with water.*

2 *ENCLOSING THE FILLING. Fold the circle in half so that the moist and dry edges meet. Press the edges firmly shut to seal them.*

3 *JOINING THE ENDS. Curl the ends round the filling and pinch these together, moistening the inner surfaces, if necessary, to make them stick. Repeat the steps with the remaining circles.*

Tortellini Stuffed with Escargots

Serves 2 (about 24 tortellini)
Working (and total) time: about 45 minutes

Calories **370**
Protein **16g**
Cholesterol **120mg**
Total fat **13g**
Saturated fat **8g**
Sodium **350mg**

	basic semolina pasta dough (page 15, but halve ingredients)	
15 g	unsalted butter	½ oz
1 tbsp	very finely chopped onion	1 tbsp
1	garlic clove, very finely chopped	1
12	giant canned snails (escargots), drained and cut in half (about 125 g/4 oz)	12
2 tsp	fresh lemon juice	2 tsp
½ tsp	chopped fresh thyme, or ¼ tsp dried thyme	½ tsp
⅛ tsp	salt	⅛ tsp
	freshly ground black pepper	
3 tbsp	finely chopped parsley	3 tbsp
4 tbsp	single cream	4 tbsp

Melt the butter in a heavy frying pan over medium heat. Add the onion and garlic and cook them, stirring often, for 3 minutes. Add the snails, lemon juice, thyme, salt and some pepper; cook for 3 minutes more, stirring frequently. Stir in the parsley and remove the pan from the heat. Transfer the snails to a small dish and refrigerate them. Stir the cream into the pan juices and set aside.

Cut the dough into two pieces. Cover one with plastic film or an inverted bowl to keep it moist. Roll out the other into a sheet about 1 mm (1/16 inch) thick *(pages 12-13)*. With a 7.5 cm (3 inch) pastry cutter, cut the sheet into 12 circles. Place a snail half slightly off centre on one of the circles. Form the round of dough into the shape of a tortellini as demonstrated above. Repeat the process with the remaining dough rounds and then with the other piece of dough.

Cook the tortellini in 3 litres (5 pints) of boiling water with 1½ teaspoons of salt until they float to the top and are *al dente* — 4 to 5 minutes. Meanwhile, heat the sauce in the frying pan. Drain the tortellini, toss them with the sauce, and serve immediately.

Fettuccine with Oysters, Spinach and Fennel

Serves 4
Working (and total) time: about 1 hour

Calories **420**
Protein **22g**
Cholesterol **140mg**
Total fat **14g**
Saturated fat **5g**
Sodium **275mg**

	basic pasta dough (page 15)	
30 g	unsalted butter	1 oz
1	fennel bulb, trimmed, cored and thinly sliced	1
4	spring onions, trimmed and thinly sliced	4
500 g	fresh spinach, washed and stemmed	1 lb
1	shallot, finely chopped	1
12.5 cl	dry white wine	4 fl oz
1 tbsp	chopped fresh tarragon, or 1 tsp dried tarragon	1 tbsp
16	oysters, shucked and drained, the liquid reserved (about 15 cl/¼ pint)	16

Roll out the dough and cut it into narrow fettuccine (pages 12-13). Set the fettuccine aside while you prepare the sauce.

In a heavy frying pan over medium-low heat, melt half the butter. Add the fennel and spring onions, cover, and cook until tender — about 10 minutes.

Meanwhile, blanch the spinach in 3 litres (5 pints) of boiling water for 40 seconds. Drain the spinach and refresh it under cold water. Squeeze the spinach dry and separate the leaves. When the fennel and spring onions finish cooking, add the spinach leaves to the pan and remove it from the heat.

In a small saucepan, combine the shallot, wine and half of the tarragon. Cook the mixture over medium-high heat until the liquid is reduced by half — about 5 minutes. Add the reserved oyster liquid and bring it to a simmer — about 3 minutes. Add the oysters to the pan and cook them just until their edges begin to curl —about 2 minutes. Reduce the heat to low to keep the oysters warm.

Cook the fettuccine in 3 litres (5 pints) of boiling water with 1½ teaspoons of salt. Start testing the pasta after 1 minute and cook it until it is *al dente*. Drain the pasta and transfer it to a large bowl. Swirl the remaining butter into the oyster sauce and combine the sauce with the pasta. Reheat the vegetables in the frying pan and stir in the remaining tarragon, then add the vegetables to the pasta and oyster sauce. Toss well and serve immediately.

Beetroot Ravioli in Soured Cream and Chive Sauce

Serves 6
Working time: about 1 hour
Total time: about 2 hours

Calories **250**
Protein **8g**
Cholesterol **55mg**
Total fat **10g**
Saturated fat **3g**
Sodium **300mg**

500 g	fresh beetroots, washed and trimmed, 5 cm (2 inch) stem left on each, or ready-cooked beetroots	1 lb
45 g	burghul	1 ½ oz
1 tbsp	white vinegar	1 tbsp
1 ½ tbsp	prepared horseradish	1 ½ tbsp
¼ tsp	salt	¼ tsp
	freshly ground black pepper	
175 to 200 g	strong plain flour	6 to 7 oz
1	egg	1
1	egg white	1
1 tbsp	safflower oil	1 tbsp
Soured cream and chive sauce		
1 tbsp	virgin olive oil	1 tbsp
1	small onion, finely chopped	1
12.5 cl	soured cream	4 fl oz
12.5 cl	plain low-fat yogurt	4 fl oz
2 tbsp	finely cut fresh chives	2 tbsp

If you are using fresh, raw beetroots, preheat the oven to 200°C (400°F or Mark 6). Tightly wrap each beetroot in aluminium foil, with the foil's dull side out. Bake the beetroots until they are tender — about 1 hour. (The beetroots may be cooked up to 24 hours ahead of time.)

Meanwhile, put the burghul in a bowl and pour 12.5 cl (4 fl oz) of boiling water over it. Let the burghul stand for at least 30 minutes.

Peel the beetroots when they are cool enough to handle. Finely chop half of the beetroots and add them to the burghul. Stir in the vinegar, ½ tablespoon of the horseradish, ⅛ teaspoon of the salt and a generous grinding of pepper. Set the mixture aside.

Cut a 2.5 cm (1 inch) thick slice from one of the remaining beetroots and purée it in a blender or food mill — it will yield about 2 tablespoons of purée. Cut the rest of the beetroots into julienne and set them aside in a warm place.

To prepare the pasta dough in a food processor, put 175 g (6 oz) of the flour, the egg, egg white, oil and beetroot purée in the bowl of the machine and process ▶

the mixture for about 30 seconds. If the mixture forms a ball immediately and is wet to the touch, mix in flour by the tablespoon until the dough feels soft but not sticky. If the mixture does not form a ball, try pinching it together with your fingers. If it is still too dry to work with, blend in water by the teaspoon until the dough just forms a ball. If you have a pasta machine, the dough may be immediately kneaded and rolled out *(pages 12-13)*.

To prepare the dough by hand, put 175 g (6 oz) of the flour in a mixing bowl and make a well in the centre. Add the egg, egg white, oil and beetroot purée to the well, and stir them with a fork or wooden spoon, gradually mixing in the flour. Transfer the dough to a lightly floured surface and knead it for a few minutes. The dough should come cleanly away from the surface; if it is too wet, add flour by the tablespoon until the dough is no longer sticky. If the dough is too dry and crumbly to work with, add water by the teaspoon until the mixture is pliable. Continue kneading the dough until it is smooth and elastic — about 10 minutes; alternatively, knead the dough with a pasta machine *(pages 12-13)*.

If you are not using a pasta machine, wrap the dough in greaseproof paper or plastic film and let it rest for 15 minutes before rolling it out.

Form the dough into ravioli *(page 18)*, filling the ravioli with the beetroot and burghul mixture.

To make the sauce, heat the oil in a heavy-bottomed saucepan over medium-high heat. Add the onion and cook it until it is translucent — about 4 minutes. Reduce the heat to low. Stir in the soured cream and yogurt and heat them through; do not let the sauce boil or the yogurt will separate. Remove the sauce from the heat, then stir in the chives, the remaining ⅛ teaspoon of salt and the remaining tablespoon of horseradish; keep the sauce warm.

Add the ravioli to 3 litres (5 pints) of boiling water with 1½ teaspoons of salt. Start testing the ravioli after 3 minutes and cook them until they are *al dente*. Drain the pasta, transfer it to a serving dish, and top it with the sauce. Distribute the julienned beetroot around the ravioli and serve the dish immediately.

Spinach Orecchiette Tossed with Cauliflower

THIS RUSTIC ITALIAN PASTA, AFFECTIONATELY CALLED "LITTLE EARS", DOES NOT REQUIRE THE USE OF A PASTA MACHINE.

Serves 4
Working (and total) time: about 1 hour and 15 minutes

Calories **315**
Protein **10g**
Cholesterol **30mg**
Total fat **13g**
Saturated fat **7g**
Sodium **275mg**

150 g	frozen spinach, thawed, or 250 g (8 oz) fresh spinach, washed, stemmed and blanched in boiling water for 1 minute	5 oz
90 g	strong plain flour	3 oz
140 g	fine semolina	4½ oz
60 g	unsalted butter	2 oz
1	small cauliflower (about 750 g/1½ lb), cored and cut into small florets	1
¼ tsp	salt	¼ tsp
1 tsp	fresh thyme, or ¼ tsp dried thyme	1 tsp
	freshly ground black pepper	
2	garlic cloves, finely chopped	2
3 tbsp	dry breadcrumbs	3 tbsp
1 tsp	chopped fresh sage, or ¼ tsp dried sage	1 tsp

To prepare the pasta dough, squeeze the spinach dry, then chop it finely. Put the flour and semolina together in a large mixing bowl. Add the spinach, then use your hands to combine it with the flours, rubbing the mixture between your fingertips to mix it evenly. Press the dough into a ball. If the dough is too dry to hold together, add a tablespoon of water and mix again. Add more water a teaspoon at a time, if necessary; the dough should be fairly dry. Knead the dough until it is smooth and elastic — about 10 minutes. Cut the dough into four pieces, then cover three of the pieces with plastic film or an inverted bowl to keep them from drying out.

Moulding Orecchiette

DIMPLING THE DOUGH. After forming a dough roll and cutting off rounds, flatten the pieces. Place a round in the palm of one hand, and indent the centre by pressing the thumb or forefinger of your other hand into it. Repeat with the other rounds.

To form the orecchiette, roll the remaining piece of dough into the shape of a rope about 1 cm (½ inch) in diameter. With a sharp knife, slice off rounds about 3 mm (⅛ inch) thick. Dip the rounds in flour to coat them lightly and make them easier to work with. Put a round in your palm and indent the centre with a finger of your other hand *(left, below)*, flattening the round to a diameter of about 2.5 cm (1 inch). Repeat the process with the remaining rounds of dough and then with the three reserved pieces.

Add the orecchiette to 3 litres (5 pints) of boiling water with 1½ teaspoons of salt. Start testing after 20 minutes and cook them until they are *al dente*.

While the pasta is cooking, heat half the butter in a large, heavy frying pan over medium-high heat. When the foam subsides, add the cauliflower florets and sauté them for 4 minutes, stirring once. Season the cauliflower with the salt, thyme and some pepper. Reduce the heat to medium and continue cooking the cauliflower until it turns golden-brown all over — 6 to 8 minutes more. Transfer the florets to a large, warmed bowl.

Reduce the heat under the pan to low. Add the remaining butter and the garlic, and cook for 15 seconds. Add the breadcrumbs, sage and more pepper; cook the breadcrumbs, stirring frequently, until they are a crisp golden-brown — about 4 minutes.

Drain the pasta, transfer it to the bowl with the cauliflower, and toss well. Scatter the breadcrumbs over the top just before serving the dish.

Tomato Fettuccine
with Artichokes and Mint

Serves 4
Working (and total) time: about 40 minutes

Tomato pasta dough		
1	egg	1
1	egg white	1
3 tbsp	tomato paste	3 tbsp
1 tbsp	virgin olive oil	1 tbsp
175 to 200 g	strong plain flour	6 to 7 oz
Artichoke and mint sauce		
6	artichokes	6
1	lemon, juice only	1
½ tsp	salt	½ tsp
	freshly ground black pepper	
4	garlic cloves, finely chopped	4
2 tbsp	chopped fresh mint or basil	2 tbsp
2 tbsp	virgin olive oil	2 tbsp

Calories **310**
Protein **9g**
Cholesterol **70mg**
Total fat **12g**
Saturated fat **2g**
Sodium **430mg**

To prepare the dough in a food processor, blend the egg, egg white, tomato paste and oil for 5 seconds. Add 175 g (6 oz) of the flour and process the mixture for about 30 seconds. If the mixture forms a ball right away and is wet to the touch, mix in flour by the tablespoon until the dough feels soft but not sticky. If the mixture does not form a ball, try pressing it into a ball with your hands. If the dough is still too dry to work with, blend in water by the teaspoon until the mixture can be formed into a ball. If you have a pasta machine, the dough may be immediately kneaded and rolled out (pages 12-13).

To prepare the dough by hand, put 175 g (6 oz) of the flour in a mixing bowl and make a well in the centre. Add the egg, egg white, tomato paste and oil to the well and mix them, gradually incorporating the flour. Transfer the dough to a lightly floured surface and knead it for a few minutes. The dough should come cleanly away from the surface; if it is too wet, add flour by the tablespoon until the dough is no longer sticky. If the dough is too dry and crumbly to work with, add water by the teaspoon until it is pliable. Continue kneading the dough until it is smooth and elastic — about 10 minutes; alternatively, knead the dough in a pasta machine (pages 12-13).

If you are not using a pasta machine, wrap the dough in greaseproof paper or plastic film and let it rest for 15 minutes before rolling it out.

After the dough is rolled out, cut it into fettuccine (page 13). Set the strips aside.

To prepare the artichokes, pour enough water into a large, non-reactive saucepan to fill it about 2.5 cm (1 inch) deep. Add the lemon juice, salt, some pepper and the garlic. Break or cut off the stalk of an artichoke. Snap off and discard the leaves, starting at the base and continuing until you reach the pale yellow leaves of the core. Using a large, sharp knife, cut through the base of the pale yellow leaves, then discard them. With a paring knife, trim away any purple leaves and the fuzzy choke, then cut the artichoke bottom into quarters. Cut each quarter into four wedges and drop them into the water in the pan. Repeat with the remaining five artichokes.

Place the pan over medium-high heat and bring the liquid to the boil. Reduce the heat and simmer the liquid until only 4 tablespoons remain and the artichokes are tender — about 15 minutes.

Meanwhile, bring 3 litres (5 pints) of water to the boil with 1½ teaspoons of salt. Add the fettuccine to the boiling water. Start testing after 2 minutes and cook the pasta until it is *al dente*. Drain the fettuccine and add it to the pan with the artichokes. Add the mint or basil and the olive oil, toss well, and serve.

Spinach Pasta Dough

Serves 4

Calories **225**
Protein **10g**
Cholesterol **60mg**
Total fat **7g**
Saturated fat **1g**
Sodium **120mg**

175 to 200 g	strong plain flour	6 to 7 oz
3 tbsp	finely chopped spinach (about 150 g/5 oz frozen spinach, thawed, or 250 g/8 oz fresh spinach, washed, stemmed and blanched in boiling water for 1 minute)	3 tbsp
1	egg	1
1	egg white	1
1 tbsp	safflower oil	1 tbsp

To prepare the dough in a food processor, purée the spinach with the egg, egg white and oil for 5 seconds. Add 175 g (6 oz) of the flour and process the mixture for about 30 seconds. If the mixture forms a ball right away and is wet to the touch, mix in flour by the tablespoon until the dough feels soft but not sticky. If the mixture does not form a ball, try pinching it together with your fingers. If it is still too dry to work with, blend in water by the teaspoon until it can be formed into a ball. If you have a pasta machine, the dough may be immediately kneaded and rolled out (pages 12-13).

To prepare the dough by hand, put 175 g (6 oz) of the flour in a mixing bowl and make a well in the centre. Add the spinach, egg, egg white and oil to the well and mix them, gradually incorporating the flour. Transfer the dough to a lightly floured surface and knead it for a few minutes. The dough should come cleanly away from the surface; if it is too wet, add flour by the tablespoon until the dough is no longer sticky. If the dough is too dry and crumbly to work with, add water by the teaspoon until it is pliable. Continue kneading the dough until it is smooth and elastic — about 10 minutes; alternatively, knead the dough in a pasta machine (pages 12-13).

If you are not using a pasta machine, wrap the dough in greaseproof paper or plastic film and let it rest for 15 minutes before rolling it out.

Crab Pillows

Serves 4
Working (and total) time: about 1 hour and 15 minutes

Calories **350**
Protein **24g**
Cholesterol **145mg**
Total fat **10g**
Saturated fat **3g**
Sodium **325mg**

	spinach pasta dough (page 29)	
350 g	crab meat, all bits of shell removed	12 oz
6	spring onions, green and white parts separated and thinly sliced	6
1½ tsp	finely chopped fresh ginger root	1½ tsp
10	drops Tabasco sauce	10
750 g	ripe tomatoes, skinned and seeded, or 400 g (14 oz) canned whole tomatoes, drained	1½ lb
1 tbsp	white wine vinegar	1 tbsp
1	garlic clove, finely chopped	1
⅛ tsp	cayenne pepper	⅛ tsp
2 tbsp	double cream	2 tbsp

To make the filling, combine the crab meat, the green spring onion parts, the ginger and the Tabasco sauce. Refrigerate the mixture.

To prepare the sauce, first purée the tomatoes in a food processor or blender. Put the purée in a saucepan. Add the vinegar, finely chopped garlic, cayenne pepper and the white spring onion parts, and bring the liquid to the boil. Reduce the heat to low and simmer the tomato sauce for 10 minutes. Set the pan aside.

Divide the pasta dough into two pieces. Roll out each piece into a strip approximately 1 mm (1/16 inch) thick and 10 cm (4 inches) wide and place the strips on a lightly floured surface *(page 13)*. Cut the strips into 12.5 cm (5 inch) lengths to form 10 by 12.5 cm (4 by 5 inch) rectangles. Spread about 2 tablespoons of the crab filling on one half of each rectangle, leaving an uncovered border about 1 cm (½ inch) wide. Moisten the edges of the rectangles lightly with your fingers, then fold the dough over the filling to form smaller rectangles that are about 6 by 10 cm (2½ by 4 inches). Press the edges firmly to seal in the filling. With a fluted pastry wheel or a knife, trim the edges. Use the dull side of a knife to press down along each of the three sealed edges; this leaves a decorative indentation and reinforces the seal.

Cook the pillows in 4 litres (7 pints) of boiling water with 2 teaspoons of salt for 5 minutes, gently turning the pillows over with a slotted spoon half way through the cooking. While the pillows are cooking, warm the sauce over low heat, then whisk in the cream. Spoon half the sauce on to a heated platter.

Remove the pillows from the boiling water with a slotted spoon, allowing most of the water to drain off. Arrange the pillows on the platter. Serve the remaining sauce separately.

Spinach Fettuccine with Chicory and Bacon

Serves 6 as an appetizer
Working (and total) time: about 30 minutes

Calories **215**
Protein **8g**
Cholesterol **50mg**
Total fat **10g**
Saturated fat **2g**
Sodium **265mg**

	spinach pasta dough (page 29)	
5	rashers lean bacon, cut into 1 cm (½ inch) pieces	5
1½ tbsp	virgin olive oil	1½ tbsp
2	large heads chicory (about 325 g/ 11 oz), ends trimmed, leaves cut diagonally into 2.5 cm (1 inch) strips and tossed with 1 tbsp fresh lemon juice	2
⅛ tsp	salt	⅛ tsp
	freshly ground black pepper	

Roll out the spinach pasta dough and cut it into fettuccine *(pages 12-13)*. Set the fettuccine aside on a lightly floured surface.

Meanwhile, cook the bacon pieces in a large, heavy frying pan over medium heat, stirring occasionally, until they are crisp — about 8 minutes. Remove the pan from the heat; with a slotted spoon, transfer the bacon pieces to a paper towel to drain. Pour off all but about 2 tablespoons of the bacon fat from the pan, and return the pan to the heat. Add the olive oil and the chicory. Sauté the chicory, stirring frequently, for 2 minutes, then sprinkle it with the salt and some pepper.

While the chicory cooks, add the fettuccine to 3 litres (5 pints) of boiling water with 1½ teaspoons of salt and cook it until it is *al dente* — about 2 minutes. Drain the pasta and add it to the chicory in the pan. Add the bacon pieces, toss well, and serve at once.

Agnolotti Filled with Turkey Mole

Serves 4 (about 36 agnolotti)
Working (and total) time: about 1 hour

Calories **445**
Protein **34g**
Cholesterol **140mg**
Total fat **14g**
Saturated fat **4g**
Sodium **370mg**

Turkey filling		
750 g	whole turkey leg, thigh skinned and boned to yield 140 g (4½ oz) of meat, the drumstick, bone and remaining meat reserved for the sauce	1½ lb
1 tbsp	safflower oil	1 tbsp
2	garlic cloves, finely chopped	2
1	onion, finely chopped	1
1	fresh hot green chili pepper, seeded and finely chopped (caution, box below)	1
¼ tsp	salt	¼ tsp
2 tbsp	chopped fresh coriander	2 tbsp
1 tbsp	grated plain chocolate	1 tbsp
Cocoa pasta dough		
175 to 200 g	strong plain flour	6 to 7 oz
1½ tbsp	cocoa	1½ tbsp
1	egg	1
1	egg white	1
Coriander sauce		
2	ripe tomatoes, skinned, seeded and chopped	2
1	garlic clove, finely chopped	1
1 tbsp	fresh lemon juice	1 tbsp
	freshly ground black pepper	
30 g	fresh coriander leaves	1 oz
1	spring onion, thinly sliced	1

Reserve the weighed turkey thigh meat. Cut the meat from the drumstick, and put it into a saucepan together with the bones and any remaining thigh meat; pour in enough water to cover them by 2.5 cm (1 inch). Cook over medium-high heat until the stock is reduced to 15 cl (¼ pint) — 30 to 45 minutes.

Meanwhile, prepare the filling. Mince the reserved turkey meat. Pour the oil into a large, heavy frying pan over low heat. Add the garlic, onion and chili pepper. Cook, stirring frequently, for 5 minutes. Add the chopped turkey meat and salt, and stir the mixture until it is well blended and the turkey's colour has begun to lighten — about 1 minute. Immediately transfer the filling to a bowl and stir in the coriander and grated chocolate. Refrigerate the filling.

To make the cocoa pasta dough in a food processor, put 175 g (6 oz) of the flour, the cocoa, egg and egg white into the bowl and process for 30 seconds. If the mixture forms a ball immediately and is wet to the touch, mix in flour by the tablespoon until the dough feels soft but not sticky. If the mixture does not form a ball, try pinching it together with your fingers. If it is still too dry to work with, blend in water by the teaspoon until the dough just forms a ball. If you have a pasta machine, the dough may be immediately kneaded and rolled out *(pages 12-13)*.

To prepare the dough by hand, mix the flour and cocoa in a bowl and make a well in the centre. Add the egg and egg white, and stir them with a fork or a wooden spoon, gradually mixing in the flour. Transfer the dough to a lightly floured surface and knead it for a few minutes. The dough should come cleanly away from the surface; if it is too wet, add flour by the tablespoon until the dough is no longer sticky. If the dough is too dry and crumbly to work with, add water by the teaspoon until it is pliable. Continue kneading the dough until it is smooth and elastic — about 10 minutes; alternatively, knead the dough in a pasta machine *(pages 12-13)*.

If you are not using a pasta machine, wrap the dough in greaseproof paper or plastic film and let it rest for 15 minutes before rolling it out.

Divide the dough into three pieces; set two of the pieces aside, covered with plastic film or an inverted bowl. Roll out the remaining piece into a sheet about 1 mm (¹⁄₁₆ inch) thick. Using a 7.5 cm (3 inch) pastry cutter, cut the sheet into about 12 circles. Place 1 teaspoon of the filling slightly off centre on each circle. Moisten the edges of the circles with water, then fold each circle in half, pressing firmly on the edges to seal in the filling. Repeat with the remaining two pieces of dough to make about 36 agnolotti.

To make the sauce, strain the reduced stock into a saucepan. Add the tomatoes, garlic, lemon juice and some pepper, and bring the liquid to the boil. Reduce the heat to low and simmer the mixture for 3 minutes. Remove the pan from the heat and stir in the coriander and spring onion.

Cook the agnolotti in 3 litres (5 pints) of boiling water with 1½ teaspoons of salt, stirring once, until the agnolotti float to the top — about 3 minutes. (If necessary to avoid overcrowding, cook the pasta in several batches.) With a slotted spoon, remove the agnolotti and keep them warm. Spoon the sauce over them just before serving.

Chili Peppers — a Cautionary Note

Both dried and fresh hot chili peppers should be handled with care. Their flesh and seeds contain volatile oils that can make skin tingle and cause eyes to burn. Rubber gloves offer protection — but the cook should still be careful not to touch the face, lips or eyes when working with chilies.

Soaking fresh chilies in cold, salted water for an hour will remove some of their fire. If canned chilies are substituted for fresh ones, they should be rinsed in cold water in order to eliminate as much of the brine used to preserve them as possible.

egg, egg white and 3 tablespoons of water. Make a well in the centre of the cornmeal mixture and pour the whisked eggs into the well. Stir the eggs, gradually incorporating the cornmeal mixture into them. When almost all of the dry ingredients are incorporated, add the olive oil and work it into the dough by hand.

Transfer the dough to a flour-dusted work surface and begin kneading it. If the dough is stiff and crumbly, add water, a teaspoon at a time; if it is too wet and sticky, gradually add flour, a tablespoon at a time, until the dough pulls away cleanly from the work surface and no longer sticks to your hands. Knead the dough until it is soft and pliable — 10 to 15 minutes. Wrap the dough in plastic film to keep it from drying out, then let it rest for 15 minutes to make it easier to roll out.

Dust the work surface with cornmeal. Remove the plastic film and roll the dough into a 60 by 23 cm (29 by 9 inch) rectangle; cut it crosswise into 1 cm (½ inch) wide strips.

To prepare the sauce, heat the safflower oil in a large, heavy frying pan over medium heat. Add the garlic and red chili peppers or crushed red pepper flakes, and cook them, stirring frequently, until the garlic turns a light brown — about 4 minutes. Add the sweet green pepper and salt, and cook for 5 minutes more. Stir in the tomato, vinegar and butter, and cook the mixture for an additional 2 minutes.

Add the dough strips to 3 litres (5 pints) of boiling water with 1½ teaspoons of salt; cover the pan. When the water returns to the boil, cook the pasta for 6 minutes. Drain the noodles and add them to the pan containing the sauce. Toss well and serve hot.

American Cornmeal Pasta with Chilies and Tomato

Serves 4
Working (and total) time: about 1 hour

Calories **295**
Protein **8g**
Cholesterol **75mg**
Total fat **12g**
Saturated fat **3g**
Sodium **265mg**

	Cornmeal pasta dough	
90 g	finely ground cornmeal	3 oz
90 g	strong plain flour	3 oz
1	egg	1
1	egg white	1
1 tbsp	virgin olive oil	1 tbsp
	Hot chili and tomato sauce	
1 tbsp	safflower oil	1 tbsp
5	garlic cloves, peeled and thinly sliced	5
2	small dried red chili peppers, finely chopped (caution, page 33), or ½ tsp crushed red pepper flakes	2
1	sweet green pepper, seeded, deribbed and chopped	1
¼ tsp	salt	¼ tsp
1	large ripe tomato, skinned, seeded and finely chopped	1
1 tbsp	red wine vinegar	1 tbsp
15 g	unsalted butter	½ oz

To make the pasta dough, mix the cornmeal and flour in a large bowl. In a small bowl, whisk together the

Buckwheat Pasta in a Sauce of Green Peppercorns and Mustard

Serves 4
Working (and total) time: about 30 minutes

Calories **375**
Protein **13g**
Cholesterol **75mg**
Total fat **11g**
Saturated fat **2g**
Sodium **385mg**

	Buckwheat pasta dough	
175 g	strong plain flour	6 oz
50 g	buckwheat flour	1¾ oz
1	egg	1
1	egg white	1
1 tbsp	safflower oil	1 tbsp
	Mustard-peppercorn sauce	
1 tbsp	safflower oil	1 tbsp
1 tbsp	finely chopped shallots	1 tbsp
12.5 cl	dry white wine	4 fl oz
2 tsp	Dijon mustard	2 tsp
1 tbsp	green peppercorns, crushed	1 tbsp
35 cl	semi-skimmed milk	12 fl oz
1	tomato, skinned, seeded and coarsely chopped	1
½ tsp	salt	½ tsp
	parsley sprigs for garnish	

To prepare the dough in a food processor, put the flours, egg, egg white and oil into the bowl of the machine and process the mixture for about 30 seconds. If the mixture forms a ball immediately and is wet to the touch, mix in flour by the tablespoon until the dough feels soft but not sticky. If the mixture does not form a ball, try pinching it together with your fingers. If it is still too dry to work with, blend in water by the teaspoon until it just forms a ball. Transfer the dough to a floured surface and knead it for a few minutes. If you have a pasta machine, use it to complete the kneading and roll out the dough *(pages 12-13)*.

To prepare the dough by hand, put the flours into a mixing bowl and make a well in the centre. Add the egg, egg white and oil to the well and stir them with a fork or wooden spoon, gradually mixing in the flour. Transfer the dough to a lightly floured surface and knead it for a few minutes. The dough should come cleanly away from the surface; if it is too wet, add flour by the tablespoon until the dough is no longer sticky. If

the dough is too dry and crumbly to work with, add water by the teaspoon until it is pliable. Continue kneading the dough until it is smooth and elastic — about 10 minutes; alternatively, knead by hand for a few minutes, then in a pasta machine *(pages 12-13)*.

If you are not using a pasta machine, wrap the dough in greaseproof paper or plastic film and let it rest for 15 minutes before rolling it out. After the dough is rolled out, cut it into fettuccine *(page 13)*.

To prepare the sauce, first heat the oil in a large, heavy-bottomed saucepan over medium-high heat. Add the shallots and sauté them until they are translucent — about 1 minute. Add the white wine, mustard and peppercorns. Cook, stirring, until almost all the wine has evaporated. Add the milk, return the mixture to a simmer, and reduce the heat to medium low. Add the noodles and simmer them in the sauce until they are *al dente* — about 3 minutes. Stir in the chopped tomato and season the dish with the salt. Garnish with the parsley and serve immediately.

Pappardelle with Turkey Braised in Red Wine

PAPPARDELLE ARE BROAD ITALIAN NOODLES. CUTTING THEM
WITH A FLUTED PASTRY WHEEL GIVES THEM THEIR
CHARACTERISTIC ZIGZAG EDGES.

Serves 8
Working time: about 1 hour and 45 minutes
Total time: about 4 hours

Calories **420**
Protein **25g**
Cholesterol **90mg**
Total fat **10g**
Saturated fat **3g**
Sodium **240mg**

	Carrot pasta dough	
250 g	carrots, peeled and thinly sliced	8 oz
200 to 225 g	strong plain flour	7 to 8 oz
1	egg	1
1	egg white	1
1 tbsp	safflower oil	1 tbsp
	Turkey sauce	
¼ tsp	fresh thyme, or ⅛ tsp dried thyme	¼ tsp
1	bay leaf	1
6	black peppercorns	6
1	clove	1
6	juniper berries, or 2 tbsp gin	6
1	onion, thinly sliced	1
1	carrot, peeled and thinly sliced	1
1	stick celery, trimmed and thinly sliced	1
3	garlic cloves, crushed	3
¾ litre	red wine, more if needed	1¼ pints
4 tbsp	brandy	4 tbsp
3	turkey drumsticks (about 350 g/12 oz each)	3
4 tbsp	plain flour	4 tbsp
1 tbsp	safflower oil	1 tbsp
175 g	mushrooms, wiped clean, quartered	6 oz
250 g	pearl onions, peeled (optional)	8 oz
4 tbsp	freshly grated Parmesan cheese	4 tbsp

To make the turkey sauce, first prepare a turkey marinade: wrap the thyme, bay leaf, peppercorns, clove and juniper berries, if you are using them, in a 10 cm (4 inch) square piece of muslin. In a large, non-reactive fireproof casserole, combine the gin (if you are using it in place of the juniper berries), the onion, carrot, celery, garlic, the bundle of seasonings and the wine. Bring the mixture to the boil, then lower the heat and simmer it for 15 minutes. Set the casserole aside; when the marinade is cool, stir in the brandy. Put the drumsticks in the casserole. (There should be enough liquid to nearly cover the legs; if there is not, pour in more wine.) Allow the drumsticks to marinate in the refrigerator for at least 2 hours.

For the pasta dough, put the carrots in a saucepan over medium-high heat and pour in enough water to cover them. Bring the water to the boil and cook the carrots until they are tender — about 7 minutes. Drain the carrots well and purée them, using a food processor, food mill or sieve. Return the purée to the saucepan and cook over medium heat, stirring constantly, to evaporate as much liquid as possible from the purée without scorching it — about 3 minutes. Set the purée aside.

If you are using a food processor to make the pasta dough, put 200 g (7 oz) of the flour, the egg, egg white, carrot purée and oil in the bowl of the machine and process the mixture for about 30 seconds. If the mixture forms a ball immediately and is wet to the touch, mix in flour by the tablespoon until the dough feels soft but not sticky. If the mixture does not form a ball, try pinching it together with your fingers. If it is still too dry to work with, blend in water by the teaspoon until the dough just forms a ball. If you have a pasta machine, the dough may be immediately kneaded and rolled out (pages 12-13).

To prepare the pasta dough by hand, put 200 g 7 oz) of the flour into a mixing bowl and make a well in the centre. Add the egg, egg white, carrot purée and oil to the well; stir them with a fork or wooden spoon, gradually mixing in the flour. Transfer the dough to a lightly floured surface and knead it for a few minutes. The dough should come cleanly away from the surface; if it is too wet, add flour by the tablespoon until the dough is no longer sticky. If the dough is too dry and crumbly to work with, add water by the teaspoon until it is pliable. Continue kneading the dough until it is smooth and elastic — about 10 minutes; alternatively, knead and roll out the dough in a pasta machine (pages 12-13).

If you are not using a pasta machine, wrap the dough in greaseproof paper or plastic film and let it rest for 15 minutes before rolling it out.

Cut the sheet of dough into pappardelle, using a fluted pastry wheel or a knife to form strips 1 to 2 cm (½ to ¾ inch) wide. (Alternatively, cut the dough into wide fettuccine.) Set the pappardelle aside.

At the end of the turkey-marinating time, preheat the grill. Remove the drumsticks from the casserole, pat the drumsticks dry with paper towels and lightly

dredge them in the flour. Brush the drumsticks with the oil and grill them about 7.5 cm (3 inches) below the heat source, turning them as they brown, for about 15 minutes. Preheat the oven to 190°C (375°F or Mark 5). Return the drumsticks to the marinade in the casserole, then place the casserole over medium-high heat and bring the marinade to the boil. Cover the casserole tightly and put it in the oven. Braise the turkey until it is tender, turning the drumsticks from time to time so that they cook evenly — about 1 hour.

About 15 minutes before the end of the braising period, put the mushrooms and the pearl onions, if using, in separate saucepans over medium-high heat and cover the vegetables with water. Bring the water to the boil and cook them until they are tender — about 3 minutes for the mushrooms, 10 minutes for the onions. Drain both pans and set them aside.

Lift the drumsticks from their sauce and put them on a plate. When they are cool enough to handle, remove the skin and discard it. Shred the turkey meat with your fingers, discarding the tendons and sinews, and set the meat aside. Remove the bundle of seasonings from the sauce and discard it. With a slotted spoon, remove the vegetables and purée them.

Skim as much fat as you can from the sauce, then combine the vegetable purée with the sauce. Stir in the turkey meat, mushrooms and, if using, the pearl onions; keep warm while you cook the pasta.

Add the pappardelle to 4 litres (7 pints) of boiling water with 2 teaspoons of salt. Start testing the pappardelle after 1 minute and cook them until they are *al dente*. Drain the pappardelle and mound them on a large heated serving dish. Pour the sauce over the pasta and serve it immediately. Pass the cheese separately.

Grated Pasta with Green Beans and Cheddar

Serves 6
Working time: about 20 minutes
Total time: about 1 hour and 20 minutes

Calories **230**
Protein **12g**
Cholesterol **60mg**
Total fat **6g**
Saturated fat **4g**
Sodium **340mg**

200 g	strong plain flour	7 oz
1	egg	1
1	egg white	1
½ tsp	salt	½ tsp
125 g	green beans, stemmed, thinly sliced on the diagonal	4 oz
½ litre	skimmed milk	16 fl oz
¼ tsp	white pepper	¼ tsp
⅛ tsp	cayenne pepper	⅛ tsp
90 g	grated Cheddar cheese	3 oz
4 tbsp	fresh breadcrumbs	4 tbsp

Put the flour in a mixing bowl and form a well in the middle of the flour. Briefly beat the egg, egg white and ¼ teaspoon of the salt in another bowl, then pour the beaten egg into the flour. Mix with a large spoon until the flour begins to form clumps. Add enough cold water (1 to 2 tablespoons) to allow you to form the mixture into a ball with your hands. Work the last of the flour into the dough by hand, then turn the dough out on to a flour-dusted surface and knead it until it is firm and smooth — about 5 minutes. Wrap the dough in plastic film and place it in the freezer for at least 1½ hours to harden it.

Remove the dough, unwrap it and grate it on the coarse side of a hand grater. Blanch the beans in boiling water for 2 minutes, then refresh them under cold running water. Preheat the oven to 180°C (350°F or Mark 4).

Bring the milk to a simmer over low heat in a large saucepan. Add the grated noodles, white pepper, cayenne pepper and the remaining ¼ teaspoon of salt. Simmer the mixture, stirring occasionally, until the noodles have absorbed almost all of the liquid — 4 to 5 minutes. Add the green beans and half of the grated cheese, and stir thoroughly.

Transfer the contents of the saucepan to an oven-proof casserole. Combine the remaining cheese with the breadcrumbs and sprinkle the mixture over the top. Bake until the crust is crisp and golden — about 20 minutes — and serve hot.

Sweet Potato Gnocchi

Serves 4
Working time: about 35 minutes
Total time: about 1 hour and 35 minutes

Calories **265**
Protein **10g**
Cholesterol **10mg**
Total fat **3g**
Saturated fat **1g**
Sodium **495mg**

500 g	sweet potatoes, baked 1 hour at 200°C (400°F or Mark 6), cooled and peeled	1 lb
4 tbsp	plain low-fat yogurt	4 tbsp
4 tbsp	freshly grated Parmesan cheese	4 tbsp
7 to 8 tbsp	strong plain flour	7 to 8 tbsp
¼ tsp	salt	¼ tsp
¼ tsp	white pepper	¼ tsp
¼ tsp	grated nutmeg	¼ tsp
¼ tsp	ground cumin	¼ tsp
3	egg whites	3
¼ litre	unsalted vegetable or chicken stock	8 fl oz
30 g	lean ham, julienned	1 oz
2 tbsp	basil leaves, cut into strips	2 tbsp

Mash the sweet potatoes in a bowl. Add the yogurt, Parmesan cheese and flour, and mix thoroughly with a fork or a wooden spoon (alternatively, put the ingredients in a blender or food processor and mix for 30 seconds, scraping the sides once). Season the mixture with the salt, pepper, nutmeg and cumin, then beat in the egg whites.

Bring 3 litres (5 pints) of water to the boil with 1½ teaspoons of salt. With two tablespoons, form the batter into oval shapes, following the instructions on the opposite page. Drop the gnocchi directly from a spoon into the boiling water, until the pot contains six or seven. When all of the gnocchi return to the surface of the water, start timing; after 3 minutes, transfer the gnocchi with a slotted spoon to a lightly oiled casserole and keep them warm. Repeat this process to cook the remaining batter.

Heat the stock and pour it over the gnocchi. Scatter the ham and basil on top. Serve at once.

Shaping Sweet Potato Gnocchi

1 *FILLING THE SPOON. Dip a tablespoon into the batter and heap a little less than a spoonful of the batter on to it. With your other hand take a second tablespoon of the same size and insert it behind the filling at a slight angle.*

2 *FORMING THE GNOCCHI. Rotate the first spoon backwards and quickly scoop the batter into the second spoon with a flick of the wrist. Scoop the batter back and forth between spoons, until the gnocchi has three flattened sides.*

3 *POACHING THE GNOCCHI. After shaping the gnocchi, dip the spoon into a pot of simmering water and stir gently. The gnocchi should come free of the spoon in seconds. Shape the rest of the gnocchi the same way, cooking six or so at a time.*

Spinach Gnocchi

Serves 4
Working time: about 40 minutes
Total time: about 1 hour

Calories **265**
Protein **18g**
Cholesterol **35mg**
Total fat **14g**
Saturated fat **6g**
Sodium **500mg**

1	medium onion, finely chopped	1
1 tbsp	virgin olive oil	1 tbsp
30 g	lean ham, chopped	1 oz
300 g	frozen spinach, thawed, or 500 g (1 lb) fresh spinach, washed, stemmed, blanched in boiling water for 1 minute and drained	10 oz
125 g	low-fat ricotta cheese	4 oz
75 g	low-fat cottage cheese	2½ oz
6 tbsp	freshly grated Parmesan cheese	6 tbsp
2	egg whites	2
⅛ tsp	grated nutmeg	⅛ tsp
60 g	strong plain flour	2 oz
15 g	unsalted butter	½ oz

In a small frying pan over medium-high heat, sauté the onion in the oil until the onion is translucent — about 2 minutes. Add the ham and sauté for 2 minutes more, then transfer the contents of the pan to a mixing bowl.

Use your hands to squeeze the spinach dry. Then chop it finely and put it in the bowl with the onion and ham.

Work the ricotta and cottage cheese through a sieve into the bowl; add 4 tablespoons of the Parmesan cheese, the egg whites, nutmeg and flour. Stir the mixture well and put it into a piping bag fitted with a 1 cm (½ inch) plain nozzle. Preheat the oven to 200°C (400°F or Mark 6).

In a large pan, bring 4 litres (7 pints) of water to the boil with 2 teaspoons of salt. Meanwhile, pipe 2.5 cm (1 inch) strips of the gnocchi mixture on to large sheets of greaseproof paper, putting about 20 gnocchi in the centre of each sheet. Pick up one of the greaseproof sheets by its edges and dip the gnocchi and paper together into the boiling water; the gnocchi will immediately separate from the paper. Discard the paper. Cook the gnocchi until they rise to the surface of the water and stay there — about 2 minutes. With a slotted spoon, transfer them to a baking dish. Cook the remaining batches of gnocchi the same way.

Dust the gnocchi with the remaining 2 tablespoons of Parmesan cheese and dot them with the butter. Bake the gnocchi until they are sizzling — about 20 minutes — and serve them immediately.

Curry Fettuccine with Chicken and Avocado

Serves 6
Working time: about 45 minutes
Total time: about 2 hours and 15 minutes

Calories **360**
Protein **25g**
Cholesterol **95mg**
Total fat **14g**
Saturated fat **2g**
Sodium **480mg**

	basic pasta dough (page 15), with 1½ tsp curry powder added to the flour	
¼ litre	plain low-fat yogurt	8 fl oz
¾ tsp	curry powder	¾ tsp
¾ tsp	salt	¾ tsp
1	garlic clove, crushed	1
5 tbsp	fresh lemon juice	5 tbsp
500 g	chicken breasts, skinned and boned	1 lb
½	avocado, peeled and cut into 1 cm (½ inch) cubes	½
350 g	carrots, peeled and sliced into 1 cm (½ inch) rounds	12 oz
	freshly ground black pepper	
2 tbsp	safflower oil	2 tbsp
2 tbsp	finely chopped parsley, preferably flat-leaf	2 tbsp

In a large, shallow bowl, combine half the yogurt, ½ teaspoon of the curry powder, ¼ teaspoon of the salt, the garlic and 3 tablespoons of the lemon juice. Arrange the chicken pieces in the bowl in a single layer and spoon the yogurt mixture over them. Let the chicken marinate in the refrigerator for at least 2 hours, turning it every 30 minutes.

Put the avocado cubes in a small bowl. Pour the remaining 2 tablespoons of lemon juice over them, then toss the cubes gently to coat them. Set aside.

Roll out the pasta dough and cut it into fettuccine *(pages 12-13)*. Set the fettuccine aside.

Put the carrots and the remaining ½ teaspoon of salt in a saucepan. Pour in just enough water to cover the carrots, then bring the water to the boil. Reduce the heat to low, cover the pan, and simmer the carrots until they are tender — 15 to 20 minutes. Drain the carrots, reserving 4 tablespoons of their cooking liquid.

In a food mill or food processor, purée the carrots with their reserved cooking liquid. Add the remaining yogurt and curry powder, and purée again. Transfer the mixture to a small saucepan and warm it over low heat. Do not let the sauce boil or the yogurt will separate.

Meanwhile, wipe the marinade from the chicken breasts and discard it. Sprinkle the chicken with some pepper. Heat the oil in a heavy frying pan over medium-high heat. Add the chicken breasts to the pan and sauté them until they are cooked through — 4 to 5 minutes on each side. Cut the meat into chunks; cover the chunks and set them aside in a warm place.

Add the fettuccine to 3 litres (5 pints) of boiling water with 1½ teaspoons of salt. Start testing the fettuccine after 1 minute and cook it until it is *al dente*.

To assemble the dish, ladle enough of the carrot purée into a heated serving dish to cover the bottom. Arrange the fettuccine on top of the purée. Spoon the remaining purée in a ring around the centre, then mound the chicken in the centre. Scatter the avocado cubes and finely chopped parsley over the chicken, and serve the dish immediately.

2 *One of the earliest (and best) of convenience foods, dried pasta fills glass storage jars in a kitchen reminiscent of pasta's Mediterranean homeland.*

The Most Varied of Foods

Dried pasta speaks Italian. Any list of available types is almost operatic in the musical sound of its Italian names — from the familiar spaghetti, linguine and lasagne to the more exotic radiatori, bucatini and fusilli. With well over a hundred shapes to tempt the cook and numberless sauces to accompany them, dried pasta ranks among the most varied of foods.

In pasta, as so often in architecture, form can follow function. All these shapes are not just intended to please the eye; many have good reason for their existence. Understanding why they look the way they do can make you a better pasta cook. Consider the spaghetti family. In addition to the familiar pasta most of us have always eaten, it includes capelli d'angelo (angel hair) and vermicelli; among its many cousins are linguine and fettuccine. Although they all share a common trait — ruler-straight lengths — they are not all to be sauced alike. The delicate capelli d'angelo and vermicelli cry out for light treatment — perhaps something as simple as chopped tomatoes, herbs and a little olive oil. The sturdier linguine and fettuccine will hold their own against a thick, strongly flavoured sauce.

Tubular pastas demand a sauce that will cling to them inside and out. Shells and dimpled shapes are exactly right for holding puddles of sauce and bits of meat or fish. Twists allow a luscious sauce to wrap itself around them, yet they will accept a light vinaigrette when served cold as a salad.

Sauce's variety is limited only by the cook's imagination. This section alone includes 53 different kinds, all of them original — from one made with Stilton cheese and port to others of spring greens and lobster, and mushrooms, yogurt and poppy seeds. At the same time as it offers such audacious combinations as these, the section takes some fresh approaches to familiar dishes. There is, for example, lasagne prepared with Gorgonzola cheese and Batavian endive. The traditional pasta with basil pesto is the inspiration for a rocket pesto, greener than its prototype yet every bit as delicious. Another dish starts with the fresh ingredients of a basil pesto — basil, pine-nuts and garlic — and instead of reducing them to a thick purée adds them directly to the pasta. The section even includes a couple of pasta dishes cooked right in the sauce. The pasta's starch thickens the sauce, while the sauce flavours the pasta. What could be easier?

A Pasta Primer

LONG THIN

SHORT TUBULAR

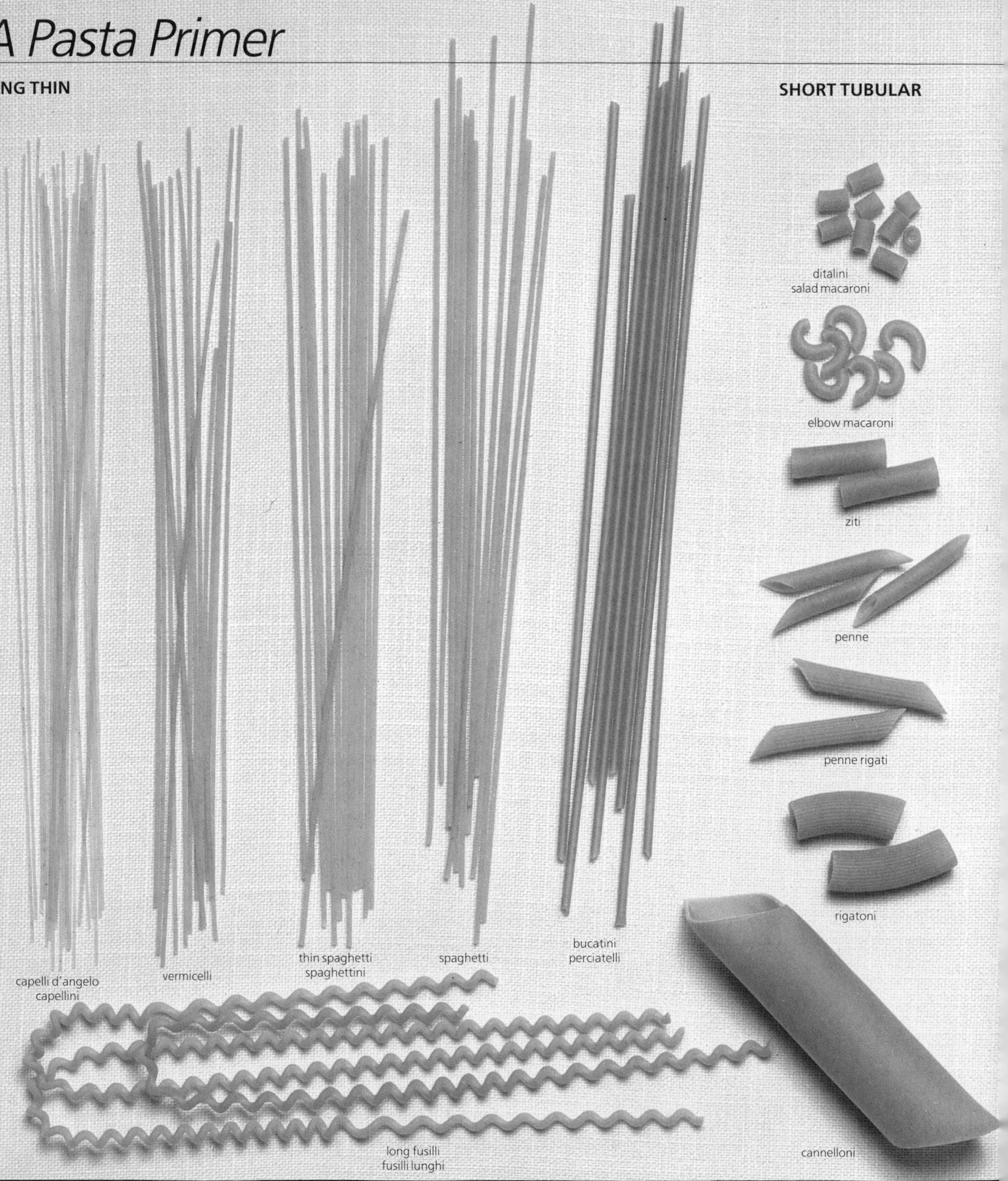

ditalini
salad macaroni

elbow macaroni

ziti

penne

penne rigati

rigatoni

capelli d'angelo
capellini

vermicelli

thin spaghetti
spaghettini

spaghetti

bucatini
perciatelli

long fusilli
fusilli lunghi

cannelloni

RIBBON

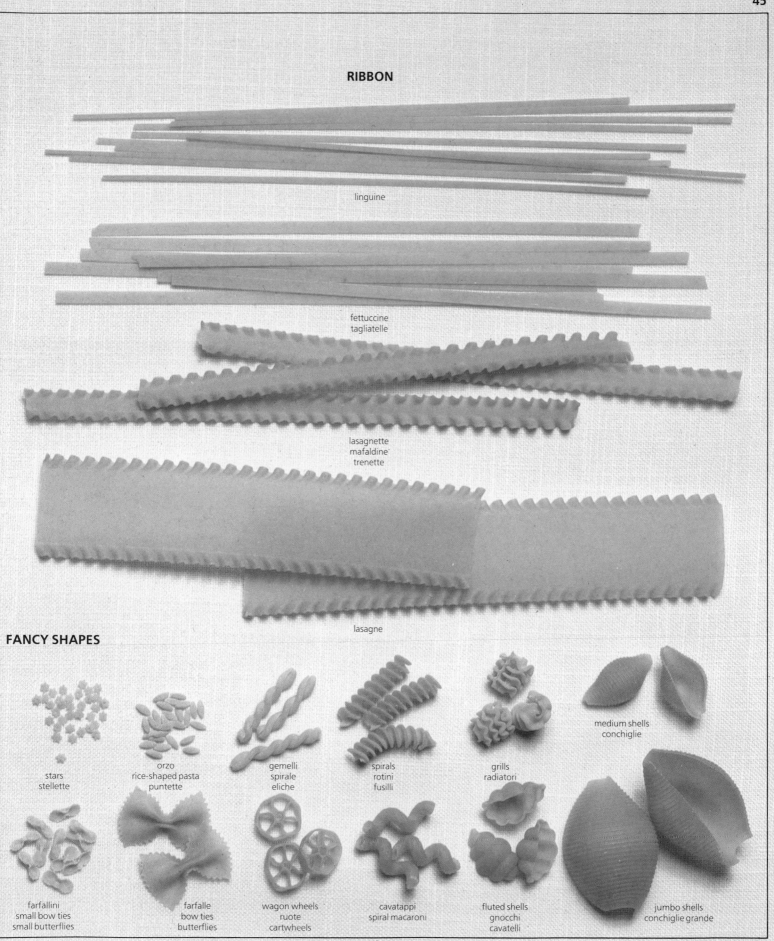

linguine

fettuccine
tagliatelle

lasagnette
mafaldine
trenette

lasagne

FANCY SHAPES

stars
stellette

orzo
rice-shaped pasta
puntette

gemelli
spirale
eliche

spirals
rotini
fusilli

grills
radiatori

medium shells
conchiglie

farfallini
small bow ties
small butterflies

farfalle
bow ties
butterflies

wagon wheels
ruote
cartwheels

cavatappi
spiral macaroni

fluted shells
gnocchi
cavatelli

jumbo shells
conchiglie grande

Linguine with Broad Beans and Grainy Mustard

Serves 4
Working (and total) time: about 20 minutes

Calories **345**
Protein **12g**
Cholesterol **15mg**
Total fat **8g**
Saturated fat **4g**
Sodium **325mg**

250 g	linguine (or spaghetti)	8 oz
250 g	ripe plum tomatoes	8 oz
17.5 cl	unsalted chicken stock	6 fl oz
165 g	fresh or frozen young broad beans	5½ oz
¼ tsp	salt	¼ tsp
2	spring onions, trimmed and thinly sliced	2
1½ tbsp	grainy mustard	1½ tbsp
30 g	unsalted butter	1 oz

Place a tomato on a cutting surface with its stem end down. With a small, sharp knife, cut wide strips of flesh from the tomato, discarding its seeds and juice. Slice each piece of tomato flesh into 5 mm (¼ inch) wide strips and set them aside. Repeat the process with the remaining tomatoes.

Pour the stock into a large, heavy frying pan over medium heat and bring it to a simmer. Add the broad beans and salt, and cook for 6 minutes. Stir in the spring onions and mustard; simmer for 1 minute more. Add the butter and the tomato strips, then simmer the mixture for an additional 2 minutes, stirring once.

Meanwhile, cook the linguine in 3 litres (5 pints) of boiling water with 1½ teaspoons of salt. Start testing the pasta after 10 minutes and cook it until it is *al dente*. Drain the linguine and transfer it to the pan with the broad bean mixture. Toss well to coat the pasta and serve immediately.

EDITOR'S NOTE: *If plum tomatoes are not available, an equivalent amount of another variety of tomato may be used.*

Penne Rigati with Mushrooms and Tarragon

Serves 4
Working (and total) time: about 45 minutes

Calories **385**	250 g	penne rigati (or other short, tubular pasta)	8 oz
Protein **11g**			
Cholesterol **0mg**	15 g	dried ceps, or porcini mushrooms	½ oz
Total fat **8g**	2 tbsp	virgin olive oil	2 tbsp
Saturated fat **1g**	1	small onion, finely chopped	1
Sodium **385mg**	250 g	button mushrooms, cut into 5 mm (¼ inch) dice	8 oz
	½ tsp	salt	½ tsp
		freshly ground black pepper	
	3	garlic cloves, finely chopped	3
	¼ litre	dry white wine	8 fl oz
	750 g	tomatoes, skinned, seeded and chopped	1½ lb
	6 tbsp	chopped parsley	6 tbsp
	2 tbsp	chopped fresh tarragon	2 tbsp

Pour ¼ litre (8 fl oz) of hot water over the dried mushrooms and soak them until they are soft — about 20 minutes. Drain the ceps and reserve their soaking liquid. Cut them into 5 mm (¼ inch) pieces.

Heat the oil in a large, heavy frying pan over medium heat. Add the onion and sauté it until it turns translucent — about 4 minutes. Add the ceps and button mushrooms, salt and pepper. Cook until the mushrooms begin to brown — about 5 minutes. Add the garlic and the wine, and cook the mixture until the liquid is reduced to approximately 2 tablespoons — about 5 minutes more.

Add the penne rigati to 3 litres (5 pints) of boiling water with 1½ teaspoons of salt. Start testing the pasta after 10 minutes and continue to cook it until it is *al dente*.

While the penne rigati is cooking, pour the reserved cep-soaking liquid into the pan containing the mushrooms and cook until the liquid is reduced to approximately 4 tablespoons — about 5 minutes. Stir in the tomatoes and cook the mixture until it is heated through — about 3 minutes more. Drain the pasta and add it to the pan along with the chopped parsley and tarragon. Toss well and serve.

Bucatini with Carrot and Courgette Serpents

Serves 6 as an appetizer
Working time: about 20 minutes
Total time: about 30 minutes

Calories **210**
Protein **6g**
Cholesterol **5mg**
Total fat **5g**
Saturated fat **1g**
Sodium **70mg**

250 g	bucatini (or linguine)	8 oz
2	carrots	2
3	medium courgettes, washed, ends removed	3
2 tbsp	virgin olive oil	2 tbsp
6	large garlic cloves, peeled, each sliced into 4 or 5 pieces	6
2	anchovy fillets, finely chopped	2
90 g	red onion, thinly sliced	3 oz
	freshly ground black pepper	

Fashion the carrot and courgette serpents: pressing down hard on a sharp vegetable peeler, grate along the length of a carrot to detach a wide strip. Continue removing strips until you reach the woody core, then turn the carrot over and repeat the process on the other side. Peel strips from the other carrot in the same manner, then cut each strip lengthwise into 5 mm (¼ inch) wide serpents. With a small, sharp knife, cut a long strip about 2.5 cm (1 inch) wide and 5 mm (¼ inch) thick from the outside of a courgette. Continue cutting strips to remove the green outer portion of all the courgettes. Discard the seedy inner cores. Cut each strip lengthwise into serpents 3 mm (⅛ inch) wide.

Put 3 litres (5 pints) of water on to boil with 1½ teaspoons of salt. Heat the oil in a large, heavy frying pan over low heat. Add the garlic slices and cook them, stirring occasionally, until they are golden-brown on both sides — 10 to 15 minutes. About 5 minutes after adding the garlic to the pan, drop the pasta into the boiling water. Start testing the pasta after 12 minutes and continue to cook it until it is *al dente*.

When the garlic slices have turned golden-brown, add the anchovy fillets, onion, carrots and courgettes to the pan; cover the pan, and cook for 3 minutes. Remove the cover and cook the mixture, stirring frequently, for 3 minutes more.

Drain the pasta and immediately add it to the pan. Add some pepper, toss well, and serve at once.

Fettuccine with Artichokes and Tomatoes

Serves 4
Working time: about 25 minutes
Total time: about 50 minutes

Calories **290**
Protein **12g**
Cholesterol **5mg**
Total fat **3g**
Saturated fat **1g**
Sodium **345mg**

250 g	fettuccine (or other narrow ribbon pasta)	8 oz
750 g	ripe tomatoes, skinned and chopped, seeds and juice reserved, or 800 g (28 oz) canned whole tomatoes, drained and chopped	1½ lb
1	onion, chopped	1
1	carrot, peeled, quartered lengthwise and cut into 5 mm (¼ inch) pieces	1
1 tsp	fresh thyme, or ¼ tsp dried thyme	1 tsp
1 tsp	chopped fresh rosemary, or ¼ tsp dried rosemary	1 tsp
¼ tsp	salt	¼ tsp
	freshly ground black pepper	
3	fresh artichoke bottoms, rubbed with the juice of 1 lemon	3
1 tbsp	red wine vinegar or cider vinegar	1 tbsp
4 tbsp	freshly grated Parmesan cheese	4 tbsp

Put the chopped tomatoes, onion, carrot, the thyme and rosemary if you are using fresh herbs, and the salt and pepper in a saucepan over medium-high heat. Bring the mixture to the boil, reduce the heat to low, and simmer the mixture for 5 minutes.

Slice the artichoke bottoms into strips 3 mm (⅛ inch) wide and add them to the pan. If you are using dried herbs, add them now. Pour in the vinegar and simmer the mixture, uncovered, for 15 minutes. Add the reserved tomato seeds and juice, if you are using fresh tomatoes, and continue cooking until most of the liquid has evaporated and the artichoke bottoms are tender but not mushy — about 15 minutes more.

Approximately 15 minutes before the vegetables finish cooking, add the fettuccine to 3 litres (5 pints) boiling water with 1½ teaspoons of salt. Start testing the pasta after 10 minutes and cook it until it is *al dente*. Drain it and add it immediately to the sauce. Sprinkle the cheese over the top, toss lightly and serve.

Sweet-and-Sour Cabbage Cannelloni

Serves 6
Working time: about 45 minutes
Total time: about 1 hour and 30 minutes

Calories **295**
Protein **9g**
Cholesterol **10mg**
Total fat **6g**
Saturated fat **3g**
Sodium **190mg**

12	cannelloni (about 250 g/8 oz)	12
30 g	unsalted butter	1 oz
1	small onion, finely chopped	1
500 g	green cabbage, shredded	1 lb
1	carrot, peeled and grated	1
1	apple, peeled, cored and grated	1
¼ tsp	salt	¼ tsp
1.25 kg	ripe tomatoes, quartered	2½ lb
1 tbsp	dark brown sugar	1 tbsp
2 tbsp	white wine vinegar	2 tbsp
4 tbsp	raisins	4 tbsp
¼ litre	unsalted chicken stock	8 fl oz

To prepare the cabbage stuffing, melt the butter in a large, heavy frying pan over medium heat. Add the onion and sauté it until it turns translucent — about 4 minutes. Pour enough water into the pan to fill it 5 mm (¼ inch) deep. Stir in the cabbage, carrot, apple and ⅛ teaspoon of the salt. Cover the pan and steam the vegetables and apple, adding more water as necessary, until they are soft — about 30 minutes. Set the pan aside.

Meanwhile, pour 4 tablespoons of water into a saucepan over medium-high heat. Add the tomatoes and cook them, stirring frequently, until they are quite soft — about 20 minutes. Transfer the tomatoes to a sieve and allow their clear liquid to drain off. Discard the liquid and purée the tomatoes into a bowl. Stir in the brown sugar, vinegar, raisins and the remaining ⅛ teaspoon of salt.

To prepare the cannelloni, add the tubes to 4 litres (7 pints) of boiling water with 2 teaspoons of salt. Start testing the cannelloni after 15 minutes and cook them until they are *al dente*. With a slotted spoon, transfer the tubes to a large bowl of cold water.

Preheat the oven to 200°C (400°F or Mark 6). Thoroughly drain the cannelloni and fill each one carefully with about one twelfth of the cabbage stuffing.

Arrange the tubes in a single layer in a large baking dish. Pour the stock over the tubes and cover the dish tightly with aluminium foil. Bake for 30 minutes. Ten minutes before serving time, transfer the sauce from the bowl to a saucepan and bring it to the boil. Reduce the heat to low and let the sauce simmer gently while the cannelloni finish cooking. Serve the cannelloni immediately; pass the sauce separately.

EDITOR'S NOTE: *To allow for cannelloni tubes that may tear during cooking or while being stuffed, add one or two extra tubes to the boiling water. The cannelloni may be assembled in advance and refrigerated for up to 24 hours before the stock is added and the dish is baked.*

Penne with Squid in Tomato-Fennel Sauce

Serves 4
Working time: about 35 minutes
Total time: about 1 hour

Calories **360**
Protein **20g**
Cholesterol **120mg**
Total fat **5g**
Saturated fat **1g**
Sodium **315mg**

250 g	penne (or other short, tubular pasta)	8 oz
350 g	squid	12 oz
1 tbsp	safflower oil	1 tbsp
4 tbsp	anise-flavoured liqueur, or 1 tsp fennel seeds	4 tbsp
750 g	tomatoes, skinned, seeded and chopped, or 400 g (14 oz) canned tomatoes, drained and chopped	1½ lb
1	fennel bulb, stalks discarded, bulb grated	1
6	spring onions, trimmed and finely chopped	6
¼ tsp	salt	¼ tsp
	freshly ground black pepper	

To clean a squid, first gently pull the quill-shaped pen out of its body pouch. Then, holding the body pouch in one hand and the head in the other, pull the two sections apart; the viscera will come away with the head. Rinse the body pouch thoroughly and rub off the thin, purplish skin covering it. Remove the triangular fins and skin them too, then slice them into strips. Cut the tentacles from the head, slicing just below the eyes. Cut out the hard beak from the centre of the tentacles and discard it. Slice the body pouch into thin rings. Repeat these steps to clean the rest of the squid.

Heat the oil in a large, heavy frying pan over medium-high heat. Sauté the squid in the oil for 1 to 2 minutes. Pour in the liqueur if you are using it, and cook the mixture for 30 seconds more. With a slotted spoon, transfer the squid to a plate. Add the tomatoes, fennel, fennel seeds if you are using them, and the spring onions to the pan. Reduce the heat to low and simmer the mixture, stirring occasionally, until the fennel is soft — 20 to 25 minutes.

When the fennel has been simmering for about 10 minutes, add the penne to 3 litres (5 pints) of boiling water with 1½ teaspoons of salt. Start testing the pasta after 10 minutes and cook it until it is *al dente*.

When the pasta is almost done, return the squid to the sauce and gently heat it through — 2 to 3 minutes. Season the sauce with the salt and the pepper. Drain the pasta, transfer it to a bowl and toss it with the sauce. Serve immediately.

Spaghetti with Fresh Basil, Pine-Nuts and Cheese

Serves 4
Working (and total) time: about 15 minutes

Calories **360**
Protein **14g**
Cholesterol **15mg**
Total fat **13g**
Saturated fat **3g**
Sodium **415mg**

250 g	spaghetti	8 oz
1 tbsp	virgin olive oil	1 tbsp
1	garlic clove, crushed	1
60 g	basil leaves, shredded, plus several whole leaves reserved for garnish	2 oz
12.5 cl	unsalted chicken stock	4 fl oz
30 g	pine-nuts, toasted in a small, dry frying pan over medium heat	1 oz
60 g	pecorino cheese, freshly grated	2 oz
¼ tsp	salt	¼ tsp
	freshly ground black pepper	

To prepare the sauce, first pour the oil into a frying pan set over medium heat. When the oil is hot, add the garlic and cook it, stirring constantly, for about 30 seconds. Reduce the heat to low. Stir in the shredded basil leaves and allow them to wilt — approximately 30 seconds. Pour in the stock and simmer the liquid gently while you cook the pasta.

Add the spaghetti to 3 litres (5 pints) of boiling water with 1½ teaspoons of salt. Start testing the pasta after 10 minutes and cook it until it is *al dente*.

Drain the pasta and add it to the pan with the basil. Toss well to coat the pasta. Add the pine-nuts, cheese, salt and some pepper, and toss again. Serve at once, garnished with the whole basil leaves.

Gorgonzola Lasagne

Serves 8
Working time: about 45 minutes
Total time: about 1 hour and 30 minutes

Calories **205**
Protein **9g**
Cholesterol **15mg**
Total fat **8g**
Saturated fat **3g**
Sodium **245mg**

250 g	lasagne	8 oz
4	sweet red peppers	4
350 g	red onions, sliced into 1 cm (½ inch) rounds	12 oz
2 tbsp	fresh lemon juice	2 tbsp
1 tbsp	fresh thyme, or ¾ tsp dried thyme	1 tbsp
2 tbsp	virgin olive oil	2 tbsp
500 g	Batavian endive, washed, trimmed and sliced crosswise into 2.5 cm (1 inch) strips	1 lb
½ tsp	salt	½ tsp
	freshly ground black pepper	
4 tbsp	freshly grated Parmesan cheese	4 tbsp
125 g	Gorgonzola cheese, broken into small pieces	4 oz

Preheat the grill. Arrange the peppers in the centre of a baking sheet with the onion slices surrounding them.

Grill the vegetables until the peppers are blistered on all sides and the onions are lightly browned — 10 to 15 minutes. (You will need to turn the peppers a few times, the onions once.) Put the peppers in a bowl, cover it with plastic film, and set it aside. Separate the onion slices into rings and reserve them as well.

Cook the lasagne in 3 litres (5 pints) of boiling unsalted water with the lemon juice for 7 minutes — the pasta will be slightly underdone. Drain the pasta and run cold water over it.

Peel the peppers when they are cool enough to handle, working over a bowl to catch the juices. Remove the stem, seeds and ribs from each pepper. Set one pepper aside and slice the remaining three into lengthwise strips about 2 cm (¾ inch) wide. Strain the pepper juices and reserve them.

Quarter the reserved whole pepper, purée the pieces in a food processor or blender with the pepper juices and 2 teaspoons of the fresh thyme or ½ teaspoon of the dried thyme. Preheat the oven to 180°C (350°F or Mark 4).

Heat the oil in a large, heavy frying pan over ▶

medium-high heat. Add the Batavian endive, ¼ teaspoon of the salt, the remaining teaspoon of fresh thyme or ¼ teaspoon of dried thyme, and a generous grinding of black pepper. Sauté the endive until it is wilted and almost all the liquid has evaporated — about 5 minutes. Remove the pan from the heat.

Line the bottom of a baking dish with a layer of the lasagne. Cover this layer with half of the endive and sprinkle it with 1 tablespoon of the Parmesan cheese. Spread half of the pepper strips over the top, then cover them with half of the onion rings. Build a second layer of lasagne, endive, Parmesan cheese, pepper strips and onion rings, this time topping the onion rings with half of the pepper purée. Cover the second level with a final layer of lasagne, and spread the remaining purée over the top. Scatter the Gorgonzola cheese evenly over the pepper sauce and sprinkle the remaining 2 tablespoons of Parmesan cheese over all.

Bake the lasagne for 30 minutes. Let the dish stand for 10 minutes to allow the flavours to meld.

Pasta Salad with Lobster and Mange-Tout

THE RADIATORI CALLED FOR HERE IS A PASTA WITH RIDGES
THAT RESEMBLE THE HEATING COILS OF A RADIATOR.
COOKING THE RADIATORI IN THE LOBSTER WATER INFUSES
THE PASTA WITH THE FLAVOUR OF THE SHELLFISH.

Serves 4
Working time: about 40 minutes
Total time: about 1 hour

Calories **375**
Protein **17g**
Cholesterol **40mg**
Total fat **12g**
Saturated fat **1g**
Sodium **270mg**

250 g	radiatori (or other fancy pasta)	8 oz
4 tbsp	very thinly sliced shallots	4 tbsp
1 tbsp	red wine vinegar	1 tbsp
3 tbsp	virgin olive oil	3 tbsp
2	garlic cloves, lightly crushed	2
¼ tsp	salt	¼ tsp
	freshly ground black pepper	
1	live lobster (about 750 g/1½ lb)	1
2 tbsp	lemon juice	2 tbsp
250 g	mange-tout, trimmed and strings removed, sliced in half with a diagonal cut	8 oz
1 tbsp	chopped fresh basil or flat-leaf parsley	1 tbsp

Pour enough water into a large pot to fill it about 2.5 cm (1 inch) deep. Bring the water to the boil and add the lobster. Cover the pot tightly and steam the lobster until it turns a bright reddish orange — about 12 minutes.

In the meantime, put half of the sliced shallots in a bowl with the vinegar and let them stand for 5 minutes.

Whisk in 2 tablespoons of the oil, then stir in the garlic, ⅛ teaspoon of the salt, and some freshly ground pepper. Set the vinaigrette aside.

Remove the lobster from the pot and set it on a dish to catch the juices. Pour 2 litres (3½ pints) of water into the pot along with 1 tablespoon of the lemon juice, and bring the liquid to the boil.

When the lobster has cooled enough to handle, twist off the tail and claws from the body. Crack the shell and remove the meat from the tail and claws. Add the shells and the body to the boiling liquid and cook for 10 minutes. Cut the meat into 1 cm (½ inch) pieces and set it aside in a bowl.

Use a slotted spoon to remove the shells from the boiling liquid; then add the pasta. Start testing after 13 minutes and cook the pasta until it is *al dente*.

While the pasta is cooking, pour the remaining oil into a large, heavy frying pan over medium-high heat. Add the mange-tout together with the remaining 2 tablespoons of shallots and ⅛ teaspoon of salt. Cook, stirring constantly, until the mange-tout turn bright green — about 1½ minutes. Scrape the contents of the pan into the bowl with the lobster.

When the pasta finishes cooking, drain it and rinse it briefly under cold water. Remove and discard the garlic from the vinaigrette, then combine the vinaigrette with the pasta. Add the lobster mixture, the basil, the remaining tablespoon of lemon juice and some more pepper, and toss well.

EDITOR'S NOTE: *Although the pasta salad may be served immediately, allowing it to stand for 30 minutes will meld its flavours. Alternatively, the salad may be served chilled.*

Pinto Beans
and Wagon Wheels

PINTO BEANS CONTAIN TOXINS CALLED LECTINS. TO DESTROY
THE LECTINS, BE SURE TO BOIL THE BEANS FOR 10 MINUTES BEFORE
ADDING THEM TO THE DISH.

Serves 4
Working time: about 25 minutes
Total time: about 9 hours and 30 minutes

Calories **575**
Protein **32g**
Cholesterol **35mg**
Total fat **13g**
Saturated fat **3g**
Sodium **470mg**

250 g	wagon wheels (or other fancy-shaped or short, tubular pasta)	8 oz
190 g	dried pinto or red kidney beans, soaked for 8 hours in water to cover and drained	6½ oz
2 tbsp	safflower oil	2 tbsp
175 g	boneless topside of beef, cut into 1 cm (½ inch) cubes	6 oz
1	small onion, finely chopped	1
1	sweet green pepper, seeded, deribbed and cut into 1 cm (½ inch) squares	1
1	garlic clove, very finely chopped	1
1.25 kg	ripe tomatoes, skinned, seeded and chopped, or 800 g (28 oz) canned whole tomatoes, drained and chopped	2½ lb
5	drops Tabasco sauce	5
1 tbsp	coarsely chopped fresh coriander	1 tbsp
	freshly ground black pepper	
½ tsp	salt	½ tsp
4 tbsp	grated Cheddar cheese	4 tbsp

Cook the beans in ¾ litre (1¼ pints) of boiling water for 10 minutes, then drain them and set them aside.

While the beans are boiling, heat the safflower oil in a large, heavy frying pan over medium-high heat. Brown the beef in the oil, stirring frequently, for 3 minutes. Remove the meat from the pan with a slotted spoon and set it aside.

Cook the onion and green pepper in the oil remaining in the pan until the onion turns translucent — about 3 minutes. Add the garlic and cook for half a minute more, then return the beef to the pan. Stir in the tomatoes, pinto beans and ¼ litre (8 fl oz) of warm water, and bring the mixture to a simmer. Cover the

pan, reduce the heat to low and simmer until the beans are tender — about 1 hour and 10 minutes.

Approximately 10 minutes before the pinto beans finish cooking, add the wagon wheels to 3 litres (5 pints) of boiling water with 1½ teaspoons of salt. Start testing the pasta after 8 minutes and continue to cook until it is *al dente*.

Drain the wagon wheels and add them to the bean mixture; stir in the Tabasco sauce, coriander, black pepper and salt. Simmer for 3 minutes more, then transfer the contents of the pan to a serving dish; sprinkle the cheese over the top and serve at once.

EDITOR'S NOTE: As a time-saving alternative to soaking the pinto beans for 8 hours, boil them in ¾ litre (1¼ pints) of water for 2 minutes, then remove the pan from the heat, cover it, and let the beans soak for 1 hour. Drain the beans and boil them in fresh water for 10 minutes, as above, before adding them to the frying pan.

Fluted Shells with Spicy Carrot Sauce

Serves 6 as an appetizer or side dish
Working time: about 15 minutes
Total time: about 1 hour

Calories **185**
Protein **7g**
Cholesterol **40mg**
Total fat **4g**
Saturated fat **2g**
Sodium **200mg**

250 g	fluted shells (or other shell-shaped pasta)	8 oz
250 g	carrots, peeled and finely chopped	8 oz
1	stick celery, finely chopped	1
4	garlic cloves, finely chopped	4
¼ tsp	crushed red pepper flakes	¼ tsp
1 tbsp	fresh thyme, or 1 tsp dried thyme	1 tbsp
½ litre	unsalted chicken or vegetable stock	16 fl oz
4 tbsp	red wine vinegar	4 tbsp
15 g	unsalted butter	½ oz
¼ tsp	salt	¼ tsp
	freshly ground black pepper	

Put the carrots, celery, garlic, red pepper flakes, thyme and enough water to cover them in a saucepan. Bring the mixture to the boil, then cover the pan and reduce the heat to medium. Simmer the vegetables until they are tender — about 20 minutes.

Pour ¼ litre (8 fl oz) of the stock into the carrot mixture and cook until the liquid is reduced to approximately 4 tablespoons — about 10 minutes. Add the remaining stock and the vinegar, and cook until only 4 tablespoons of liquid remain — about 10 minutes more.

While you are reducing the second portion of stock, cook the pasta in 3 litres (5 pints) of boiling water with 1½ teaspoons of salt. Start testing the pasta after 5 minutes and cook it until it is *al dente*.

Stir the butter, salt and pepper into the sauce. Drain the pasta, put it in a bowl, and toss it with the sauce.

Chilled Spirals with Rocket Pesto

Serves 4
Working time: about 25 minutes
Total time: about 2 hours

Calories **535**
Protein **17g**
Cholesterol **10mg**
Total fat **22g**
Saturated fat **4g**
Sodium **395mg**

350 g	spirals	12 oz
125 g	rocket, washed, cleaned and stemmed	4 oz
1	small garlic clove, coarsely chopped	1
30 g	pine-nuts	1 oz
3 tbsp	virgin olive oil	3 tbsp
1 tbsp	safflower oil	1 tbsp
60 g	Parmesan cheese, freshly grated	2 oz
¼ tsp	salt	¼ tsp
	freshly ground black pepper	
1	sweet red pepper, seeded, deribbed and finely diced	1
2 tbsp	balsamic vinegar, or 1 tbsp red wine vinegar	2 tbsp

Add the spirals to 4 litres (7 pints) of boiling water with 2 teaspoons of salt. Start testing the pasta after 8 minutes and cook it until it is *al dente*.

Meanwhile, prepare the pesto: put the rocket, garlic, pine-nuts, olive oil and safflower oil in a blender or food processor. Blend for 2 minutes, stopping two or three times to scrape down the sides. Add the cheese and the salt; blend the mixture briefly to form a purée.

Drain the pasta, transfer it to a large bowl, and season it with some black pepper. Add the diced red pepper, the vinegar and pesto, and toss well. Chill the pasta salad in the refrigerator for 1 to 2 hours before serving it.

Ziti with Italian Sausage and Red Peppers

Serves 4
Working time: about 30 minutes
Total time: about 40 minutes

Calories **300**
Protein **11g**
Cholesterol **10mg**
Total fat **7g**
Saturated fat **2g**
Sodium **330mg**

250 g	ziti (or other tubular pasta)	8 oz
3	sweet red peppers	3
125 g	spicy Italian pork sausages	4 oz
2	garlic cloves, finely chopped	2
2 tsp	fresh thyme, or ½ tsp dried thyme	2 tsp
1	large tomato, skinned, seeded and puréed	1
1 tbsp	red wine vinegar	1 tbsp
⅛ tsp	salt	⅛ tsp

Preheat the grill. Place the peppers 5 cm (2 inches) below the heat source, turning them from time to time, until they are blackened all over — 15 to 18 minutes. Put the peppers in a bowl and cover it with plastic film. The trapped steam will loosen their skins.

Squeeze the sausages out of their casings and break the meat into small pieces; sauté the pieces over medium-high heat until they are browned — about 3 minutes. Remove the pan from the heat and stir in the garlic and the thyme.

Add the pasta to 3 litres (5 pints) of boiling water with 1½ teaspoons of salt; start testing it after 10 minutes and cook it until it is *al dente*.

While the pasta is cooking, peel the peppers, working over a bowl to catch the juices. Remove and discard the stems, seeds and ribs; strain the juices and reserve them. Slice the peppers lengthwise into thin strips.

Set the pan containing the sausage mixture over medium heat. Add the pepper strips and their reserved juices, the puréed tomato, the vinegar and the ⅛ teaspoon of salt. Simmer the sauce until it thickens and is reduced by about one third — 5 to 7 minutes.

Drain the pasta, return it to the pan, and combine it with the sauce. Cover the pan and let the pasta stand for 5 minutes to allow the flavours to blend.

Vermicelli,
Onions and Peas

Serves 8 as a side dish
Working time: about 15 minutes
Total time: about 1 hour

Calories **185**
Protein **5g**
Cholesterol **0mg**
Total fat **4g**
Saturated fat **1g**
Sodium **120mg**

250 g	vermicelli or spaghettini	8 oz
2 tbsp	virgin olive oil	2 tbsp
500 g	onions, chopped	1 lb
1	leek, trimmed, cleaned and thinly sliced	1
¼ tsp	salt	¼ tsp
	freshly ground black pepper	
¼ litre	dry white wine	8 fl oz
75 g	shelled peas	2½ oz

Heat the oil in a large, heavy frying pan over low heat. Add the onions, leek, salt and a generous grinding of pepper. Cover the pan tightly and cook, stirring frequently to keep the onions from sticking, until the vegetables are very soft — about 45 minutes.

Cook the pasta in 3 litres (5 pints) of boiling water with 1½ teaspoons of salt. Start testing the pasta after 7 minutes and cook it until it is *al dente*.

While the pasta is cooking, finish the sauce: pour the wine into the pan and raise the heat to high. Cook

the mixture until the liquid is reduced to about 4 tablespoons — approximately 5 minutes. Stir in the peas, cover the pan, and cook for another 1 to 2 minutes to heat the peas through. If you are using fresh peas, increase the cooking time to 5 minutes.

Drain the pasta and transfer it to a serving dish; pour the contents of the frying pan over the top and toss well. Serve immediately.

Lasagne Roll-Ups

Serves 6
Working time: about 45 minutes
Total time: about 1 hour and 10 minutes

Calories **445**
Protein **24g**
Cholesterol **35mg**
Total fat **16g**
Saturated fat **7g**
Sodium **340mg**

12	lasagne strips	12
500 g	low-fat ricotta cheese	1 lb
125 g	low-fat mozzarella, shredded	4 oz
250 g	broccoli, steamed for 5 minutes, drained and chopped	8 oz
75 g	mushrooms, sliced	2½ oz
2	spring onions, trimmed and chopped	2
2 tbsp	chopped fresh basil, or 2 tsp dried basil	2 tbsp
1 tbsp	chopped fresh oregano, or 1 tsp dried oregano	1 tbsp
4 tbsp	chopped parsley	4 tbsp
Tomato sauce		
2 tbsp	safflower oil	2 tbsp
1	onion, coarsely chopped	1
2	small carrots, peeled and coarsely chopped	2
2	sticks celery, trimmed and coarsely chopped	2
2	garlic cloves, thinly sliced	2
3 tbsp	chopped fresh basil, or 1 tbsp dried basil	3 tbsp
	freshly ground black pepper	
1	bay leaf	1
15 cl	Madeira	¼ pint
1.25 kg	ripe tomatoes, skinned, seeded and chopped, or 800 g (28 oz) canned whole tomatoes, drained and chopped	2½ lb
2 tbsp	tomato paste	2 tbsp
125 g	unsweetened apple purée	4 oz
3 tbsp	freshly grated Parmesan cheese	3 tbsp

To make the sauce, pour the oil into a large, heavy-bottomed saucepan over medium-high heat. Add the onion, carrots and celery. Sauté the mixture, stirring frequently, for 2 minutes. Add the garlic and cook for 1 minute more. Stir in the basil, pepper, bay leaf and Madeira. Bring the liquid to the boil and cook it until it is reduced by about half — 2 to 3 minutes. Add the tomatoes, tomato paste and apple purée. As soon as the liquid returns to the boil, reduce the heat to low and gently simmer the sauce for 30 to 35 minutes. Remove the bay leaf and transfer the sauce to a food processor or blender. Purée the sauce and return it to the saucepan. Stir in the grated Parmesan cheese and set the pan aside.

Preheat the oven to 180°C (350°F or Mark 4). Add the lasagne to 4 litres (7 pints) of boiling water with 2 teaspoons of salt. Start testing the pasta after 12 minutes and cook it until it is *al dente*. Drain the pieces and spread them on a clean tea towel to dry.

In a large bowl, mix the ricotta, mozzarella, broccoli, mushrooms, spring onions, basil, oregano and parsley.

To assemble the dish, spread ¼ litre (8 fl oz) of the tomato sauce over the bottom of a 28 by 33 cm (11 by 13 inch) baking dish. Spread about 4 tablespoons of the cheese and vegetable mixture over a lasagne strip; starting at one end, roll up the strip. Place the roll, seam side down, in the dish. Repeat with the remaining lasagne strips and filling. Pour the rest of the sauce over the rolls and cover the pan tightly with aluminium foil. Bake the rolls for 20 minutes, then remove the foil and bake them for 15 to 20 minutes more. Serve piping hot.

EDITOR'S NOTE: *To compensate for lasagne that may tear during cooking, add one or two extra strips to the boiling water.*

Vermicelli Salad with Sliced Pork

Serves 6
Working (and total) time: about 30 minutes

Calories **205**
Protein **9g**
Cholesterol **15mg**
Total fat **3g**
Saturated fat **1g**
Sodium **235mg**

250 g	vermicelli (or other long, thin pasta)	8 oz
½ tbsp	safflower oil	½ tbsp
125 g	pork loin, fat trimmed, meat pounded flat and sliced into thin strips	4 oz
2	garlic cloves, finely chopped	2
3	carrots, peeled and julienned	3
4	sticks celery, trimmed and julienned	4
2 tsp	dark sesame oil	2 tsp
¼ tsp	salt	¼ tsp
	freshly ground black pepper	
6	drops Tabasco sauce	6
2 tbsp	rice vinegar	2 tbsp
1 tsp	sweet sherry	1 tsp

Break the vermicelli into thirds and drop it into 3 litres (5 pints) of boiling water with 1½ teaspoons of salt. Start testing the pasta after 5 minutes and continue to cook it until it is *al dente*.

While the pasta is cooking, heat the safflower oil in a wok or a large frying pan over medium-high heat. Stir-fry the pork strips in the oil for 2 minutes. Add the garlic and cook for 30 seconds, stirring constantly to keep it from burning. Add the carrots and celery, and stir-fry the mixture for 2 minutes more.

Drain the pasta and toss it in a large bowl with the pork and vegetable mixture. Dribble the sesame oil over the pasta, then sprinkle it with the ¼ teaspoon of salt, the black pepper and the Tabasco sauce, and toss thoroughly. Pour the vinegar and sherry over the salad and toss it once more. Serve the salad at room temperature or chilled.

Penne with Smoked Pork and Mushroom Sauce

Serves 8
Working time: about 15 minutes
Total time: about 45 minutes

Calories **315**
Protein **11g**
Cholesterol **5mg**
Total fat **6g**
Saturated fat **2g**
Sodium **215mg**

500 g	penne (or other short, tubular pasta)	1 lb
1.25 kg	Italian plum tomatoes, quartered, or 800 g (28 oz) canned whole tomatoes, drained	2½ lb
4	whole dried red chili peppers	4
2 tbsp	virgin olive oil	2 tbsp
1	onion, finely chopped	1
500 g	mushrooms, wiped clean and sliced	1 lb
60 g	smoked pork loin or smoked back bacon, julienned	2 oz
4	garlic cloves, finely chopped	4
12.5 cl	dry white wine	4 fl oz
2 tbsp	chopped parsley, preferably flat-leaf	2 tbsp
15 g	unsalted butter	½ oz

for 2 minutes, then add the pork and garlic and sauté for 2 minutes more. Pour in the wine and cook the mixture until the liquid is reduced by half — about 3 minutes. Stir in the reserved tomato mixture and the parsley, and keep the sauce warm.

Drain the penne and transfer it to a serving dish. Toss it with the butter and the sauce and serve.

In a large saucepan, combine the tomatoes, chili peppers and 4 tablespoons of water. Cook over medium heat until the tomatoes have rendered their juice and most of the liquid has evaporated — about 20 minutes. Work the mixture through a sieve and set it aside.

Add the penne to 3 litres (5 pints) of boiling water with 1½ teaspoons of salt. Begin testing the pasta after 10 minutes and cook it until it is *al dente*.

While the pasta is cooking, heat the oil in a large frying pan over medium-high heat. Add the onion and sauté it, stirring constantly, until it turns translucent — about 3 minutes. Add the mushrooms and sauté them

Macaroni Baked with Stilton and Port

Serves 6
Working time: about 20 minutes
Total time: about 45 minutes

Calories **300**
Protein **11g**
Cholesterol **15mg**
Total fat **9g**
Saturated fat **4g**
Sodium **400mg**

250 g	elbow macaroni	8 oz
1 tbsp	safflower oil	1 tbsp
2	shallots, finely chopped	2
2 tbsp	flour	2 tbsp
12.5 cl	ruby port	4 fl oz
¼ litre	semi-skimmed milk	8 fl oz
¼ litre	unsalted chicken stock	8 fl oz
125 g	Stilton, crumbled	4 oz
2 tsp	Dijon mustard	2 tsp
⅛ tsp	white pepper	⅛ tsp
4 tbsp	dry breadcrumbs	4 tbsp
1 tsp	paprika	1 tsp

Preheat the oven to 180°C (350°F or Mark 4). Pour the oil into a large, heavy-bottomed saucepan over medium heat. Add the shallots and cook them, stirring occasionally, until they are transparent — approximately 2 minutes. Sprinkle the flour over the shallots and cook the mixture, stirring continuously, for 2 minutes more.

Pour the port into the pan and whisk slowly; add the milk and the stock in the same manner, whisking after each addition, to form a smooth sauce. Gently simmer the sauce for 3 minutes. Stir in half of the cheese along with the mustard and pepper. Continue stirring until the cheese has melted.

Meanwhile, cook the macaroni in 3 litres (5 pints) of boiling water with 1½ teaspoons of salt. Start testing the pasta after 10 minutes and cook it until it is al dente.

Drain the macaroni and combine it with the sauce, then transfer the mixture to a baking dish. Combine the breadcrumbs with the remaining crumbled cheese and scatter the mixture evenly over the top. Sprinkle the paprika over all and bake the dish until the sauce is bubbling hot and the top is crisp — 20 to 25 minutes. Serve immediately.

Spirals with Lemon Sauce and Dill

Serves 4
Working (and total) time: about 20 minutes

Calories **290**
Protein **9g**
Cholesterol **10mg**
Total fat **3g**
Saturated fat **1g**
Sodium **100mg**

250 g	spirals	8 oz
¼ litre	milk	8 fl oz
⅛ tsp	salt	⅛ tsp
4 tbsp	aquavit, or 4 tbsp vodka and 1 tsp caraway seeds	4 tbsp
3 tbsp	fresh lemon juice	3 tbsp
5 cm	strip of lemon rind	2 inch
2 tbsp	finely cut fresh dill, or 2 tsp dried dill	2 tbsp

Put the milk, salt, aquavit or vodka and caraway seeds, lemon juice and lemon rind in a large non-stick or heavy frying pan. Bring the liquid to the boil, reduce the heat and simmer gently for 3 minutes. Add the spirals and enough water to almost cover them. Cover the pan and cook over low heat, removing the lid and stirring occasionally, until the spirals are *al dente* and about 4 tablespoons of sauce remains — approximately 15 minutes. (If necessary, add more water to keep the spirals from sticking.) Remove the lemon rind and discard it. Stir in the chopped dill and serve the dish immediately.

Linguine with Mussels in Saffron Sauce

Serves 4
Working (and total) time: about 30 minutes

Calories **475**
Protein **23g**
Cholesterol **30mg**
Total fat **8g**
Saturated fat **2g**
Sodium **560mg**

350 g	linguine (or spaghetti)	12 oz
1 kg	large mussels, scrubbed and debearded	2 lb
1 tbsp	safflower oil	1 tbsp
1	shallot, finely chopped	1
2 tbsp	flour	2 tbsp
12.5 cl	dry vermouth	4 fl oz
⅛ tsp	saffron threads, steeped in 17.5 cl (6 fl oz) hot water	⅛ tsp
4 tbsp	freshly grated pecorino cheese	4 tbsp
¼ tsp	salt	¼ tsp
	freshly ground black pepper	
1 tbsp	cut chives	1 tbsp

Put the mussels and 12.5 cl (4 fl oz) of water in a large pan. Cover the pan and steam the mussels over high heat until they open — about 5 minutes. Remove the mussels from the pan with a slotted spoon and set them aside. Discard any mussels that do not open.

When the mussels are cool enough to handle, remove the meat from the shells, working over the pan to catch any liquid; set the meat aside and discard the shells. Strain the liquid left in the bottom of the pan through a very fine sieve. Set the liquid aside.

Heat the safflower oil in a heavy frying pan over medium-high heat. Add the finely chopped shallot and sauté it for 30 seconds. Remove the pan from the heat. Whisk in the 2 tablespoons of flour, then the dry vermouth and the saffron liquid (whisking prevents lumps from forming). Return the frying pan to the

heat and simmer the sauce over medium-low heat until it thickens — 2 to 3 minutes.

Meanwhile, cook the linguine in 3 litres (5 pints) of boiling water with 1½ teaspoons of salt. Start testing the pasta after 10 minutes and cook it until it is *al dente*.

To finish the sauce, stir in 4 tablespoons of the strained mussel-cooking liquid along with the cheese, salt, pepper, chives and mussels. Simmer the sauce for 3 to 4 minutes more to heat the mussels through.

Drain the linguine, transfer it to a bowl and toss it with the sauce. Serve immediately.

Linguine Sauced with Capers, Black Olives and Tomatoes

Serves 4
Working (and total) time: about 35 minutes

Calories **300**
Protein **10g**
Cholesterol **5mg**
Total fat **6g**
Saturated fat **1g**
Sodium **485mg**

250 g	linguine (or spaghetti)	8 oz
1	garlic clove, very finely chopped	1
1 tbsp	safflower oil	1 tbsp
1.25 kg	ripe tomatoes, skinned, seeded and chopped, or 800 g (28 oz) canned whole tomatoes, drained and chopped	2½ lb
2 tsp	capers, drained and chopped	2 tsp
6	black olives, stoned and cut lengthwise into strips	6
⅛ tsp	crushed red pepper flakes	⅛ tsp
¼ tsp	salt	¼ tsp
1 tsp	chopped fresh oregano, or ½ tsp dried oregano	1 tsp
2 tbsp	freshly grated pecorino cheese	2 tbsp

In a large, heavy frying pan over medium heat, cook the garlic in the oil for 30 seconds. Add the tomatoes, capers, olives, red pepper flakes and salt. Reduce the heat to low, partially cover the pan and cook the mixture for 20 minutes. Add the oregano and cook for 10 minutes more.

About 10 minutes before the sauce finishes cooking, add the linguine to 3 litres (5 pints) of boiling water with 1½ teaspoons of salt. Start testing the linguine after 10 minutes and cook it until it is *al dente*. Drain the pasta and add it to the sauce. Mix well together to coat the pasta with the sauce. Sprinkle the grated cheese on top before serving.

Shells Stuffed with Crab Meat and Spinach

Serves 6

Working time: about 30 minutes

Total time: about 45 minutes

Calories **220**
Protein **14g**
Cholesterol **50mg**
Total fat **8g**
Saturated fat **2g**
Sodium **365mg**

12	giant pasta shells, each about 6 cm (2¼ inches) long	12
2 tbsp	safflower oil	2 tbsp
1	large onion, chopped	1
⅛ tsp	salt	⅛ tsp
	freshly ground black pepper	
125 g	fresh spinach, stemmed, washed and sliced into a chiffonade	4 oz
1 tbsp	chopped fresh basil or flat-leaf parsley	1 tbsp
2 tbsp	fresh lime juice	2 tbsp
350 g	fresh crab meat, picked over and flaked	12 oz
125 g	low-fat ricotta	4 oz
White wine sauce		
12.5 cl	dry white wine	4 fl oz
1 tbsp	finely chopped shallot	1 tbsp
⅛ tsp	salt	⅛ tsp
	freshly ground black pepper	
1 tbsp	chopped fresh basil or flat-leaf parsley	1 tbsp
1 tbsp	double cream	1 tbsp

Preheat the oven to 180°C (350°F or Mark 4). Cook the shells in 4 litres (7 pints) of boiling water with 1 teaspoon of salt, stirring gently to prevent sticking, for 12 minutes — they will be slightly undercooked. Drain the shells and rinse them under cold running water.

While the pasta is cooking, heat 1 tablespoon of the oil in a heavy frying pan over medium heat. Add the onion, salt and pepper, and cook, stirring frequently, until the onion begins to brown — about 10 minutes. Stir in the spinach, the basil or parsley, and 1 tablespoon of the lime juice. Cook the mixture, stirring, until the spinach wilts — about 2 minutes.

Remove the pan from the heat. Add the crab meat, the ricotta, the remaining tablespoon of lime juice and some more pepper; mix lightly.

Stuff each shell with some of the crab meat mixture, gently pressing it down to round out the shell.

Put the shells in a shallow baking dish and dribble the remaining oil over them. Cover loosely with aluminium foil, shiny side down, and bake for 20 minutes.

While the shells are baking, prepare the sauce. Put the white wine, shallot, salt, pepper and 12.5 cl (4 fl oz) of water in a small saucepan. Bring the mixture to the boil, then reduce the heat to medium-low and simmer until only about 6 tablespoons of liquid remain — 12 to 15 minutes. Remove the pan from the heat; add the basil or parsley, and whisk in the cream. Return the pan to the heat and cook the sauce for 2 to 3 minutes more to thicken it slightly.

Pour the sauce over the baked shells and serve.

EDITOR'S NOTE: *To compensate for shells that may tear during cooking, add one or two extra shells to the boiling water.*

Orzo and Wild Mushrooms

Serves 4 as an appetizer or side dish
Working time: about 30 minutes
Total time: about 40 minutes

Calories **255**
Protein **8g**
Cholesterol **10mg**
Total fat **4g**
Saturated fat **2g**
Sodium **165mg**

200 g	orzo	7 oz
30 g	dried ceps or other wild mushrooms, soaked in ¼ litre (8 fl oz) hot water for 20 minutes	1 oz
15 g	unsalted butter	½ oz
35 cl	unsalted chicken stock	12 fl oz
1	garlic clove, finely chopped	1
1 tsp	fresh thyme, or ¼ tsp dried thyme	1 tsp
¼ tsp	salt	¼ tsp
	freshly ground black pepper	

Remove the mushrooms from their soaking liquid and slice them into thin strips. Strain the liquid through a fine-meshed sieve and reserve 12.5 cl (4 fl oz) of it.

Melt the butter in a heavy-bottomed saucepan over medium heat. Add the pasta and the sliced mushrooms to the pan and cook the mixture for 5 minutes, stirring frequently. Add the reserved mushroom-soaking liquid, 12.5 cl (4 fl oz) of the stock, the garlic, thyme, salt and pepper. Cook, stirring all the while, until the orzo has absorbed most of the liquid — 7 to 8 minutes.

Reduce the heat to low and pour in another 12.5 cl (4 fl oz) of stock; cook, stirring constantly, until the liquid has been absorbed — 3 to 4 minutes. Repeat this process once more with the remaining stock, cooking the mixture until the pasta is tender but still moist. Serve the dish immediately.

Star-Stuffed Peppers

Serves 4
Working time: about 45 minutes
Total time: about 1 hour and 15 minutes

Calories **380**
Protein **17g**
Cholesterol **25mg**
Total fat **10g**
Saturated fat **1g**
Sodium **350mg**

250 g	stellette (stars)	8 oz
150 g	skinned, boneless chicken breast, meat cut into small pieces	5 oz
3	spring onions, trimmed and thinly sliced	3
1	large garlic clove, crushed	1
1½ tbsp	coarsely chopped fresh ginger root	1½ tbsp
2 tbsp	safflower oil	2 tbsp
90 g	canned pimientos, drained, finely chopped	3 oz
	freshly ground black pepper	
2 tsp	white vinegar	2 tsp
½ tsp	salt	½ tsp
4	sweet green peppers, or very mild, large green chili peppers (about 15 cm/ 6 inches long)	4
1 tsp	dark sesame oil	1 tsp

To prepare the stuffing, mound the chicken pieces, spring onions, garlic and ginger together on a cutting board and chop them into fine pieces.

Heat the safflower oil in a large, heavy frying pan over medium heat. Add the chicken mixture to the pan; sauté the mixture, breaking it up and turning it frequently with a spatula or wooden spoon, until the meat has turned white — about 4 minutes. Stir in the chopped pimientos, black pepper, vinegar and ¼ teaspoon of the salt.

Add the stellette to 2 litres (3½ pints) of boiling water with ½ teaspoon of salt. Start testing them after 2 minutes and cook them until they are *al dente*. Drain them and stir them into the chicken mixture.

Preheat the oven to 180°C (350°F or Mark 4). Slice off the peppers' tops and set them aside; with a small spoon, scoop the seeds and the ribs from inside the cavities. Dip a finger into the sesame oil and rub it over the insides of the peppers, then sprinkle the insides with the remaining ¼ teaspoon of salt. Fill the peppers with the chicken stuffing and replace their tops; reserve the stuffing that is left over.

Lightly oil a shallow baking dish and arrange the stuffed peppers in it in a single layer. Bake the peppers for 25 minutes. Remove the dish from the oven and distribute the reserved stuffing around the peppers. Return the dish to the oven for 5 minutes before serving the peppers.

Long Fusilli with Chanterelles

Serves 2
Working (and total) time: about 25 minutes

Calories **360**
Protein **10g**
Cholesterol **15mg**
Total fat **14g**
Saturated fat **5g**
Sodium **380mg**

125 g	long fusilli (or fettuccine or other narrow ribbon pasta)	4 oz
1	ripe tomato	1
1 tbsp	virgin olive oil	1 tbsp
15 g	unsalted butter	½ oz
165 g	chanterelles or oyster mushrooms, wiped clean, trimmed and thinly sliced	5½ oz
¼ tsp	salt	¼ tsp
	freshly ground black pepper	
1	garlic clove, finely chopped	1
1½ tbsp	finely cut chives or spring onions	1½ tbsp

Place the tomato on a cutting surface with its stem end down. With a sharp knife, cut wide pieces of flesh from the tomato, discarding the seeds and juices. Slice each piece of flesh into very thin strips and set them aside.

Cook the fusilli in 2 litres (3½ pints) of boiling water with 1 teaspoon of salt. Start testing the pasta after 10 minutes and cook it until it is *al dente*.

While the pasta is cooking, heat the oil and butter in a large, heavy frying pan over medium heat. Add the chanterelles or oyster mushrooms, the salt and some pepper, and sauté them for 3 minutes, stirring occasionally. Add the garlic, 1 tablespoon of the chives or spring onions, and the tomato. Sauté for 2 minutes more.

Drain the pasta, add it to the pan with the mushroom mixture, and toss well. Serve the dish immediately, garnished with the remaining ½ tablespoon of chives or spring onions.

Orzo and Mussels

Serves 4
Working time: about 30 minutes
Total time: about 40 minutes

Calories **400**
Protein **17g**
Cholesterol **20mg**
Total fat **9g**
Saturated fat **1g**
Sodium **390mg**

250 g	orzo (or other small pasta)	8 oz
1	orange	1
2 tbsp	virgin olive oil	2 tbsp
1	onion, finely chopped	1
4	garlic cloves, finely chopped	4
1 kg	tomatoes, skinned, seeded and finely chopped	2 lb
2 tsp	fennel seeds	2 tsp
1½ tbsp	tomato paste	1½ tbsp
12.5 cl	dry vermouth	4 fl oz
¼ tsp	salt	¼ tsp
3 tbsp	chopped fresh parsley, or 1 tbsp dried parsley	3 tbsp
1 tsp	fresh thyme, or ¼ tsp dried thyme	1 tsp
750 g	mussels, scrubbed and debearded	1½ lb

With a sharp knife, pare the rind from the orange and cut it into tiny julienne. Put the strips in a small saucepan with ¼ litre (8 fl oz) of cold water. Bring the water to the boil, then remove the pan from the heat. Rinse the rind under cold running water and set it aside. Squeeze the juice from the orange and reserve it as well.

Heat the oil in a large fireproof casserole over medium heat. Add the chopped onion and cook it for 3 minutes, stirring constantly. Add the chopped garlic and cook, stirring, until the onion is translucent — about 2 minutes more.

Push the onion-garlic mixture to one side of the casserole. Add the tomatoes and the fennel seeds, and raise the heat to high. Cook the tomatoes just enough to soften them without destroying their texture — approximately 1 minute. Stir the onion-garlic mixture in with the tomatoes. Add the tomato paste, orange juice, vermouth and salt to the casserole, and stir well. Reduce the heat to medium and simmer the sauce for 5 minutes. Add the parsley, thyme and orange rind.

Place the mussels on top of the sauce. Cover the casserole and steam the mussels until they open — 3 to 5 minutes. If any mussels remain closed, discard them. Remove the casserole from the heat and set it aside with its lid on to keep the contents warm.

Add the orzo to 3 litres (5 pints) of boiling water with 1½ teaspoons of salt. Start testing after 10 minutes and cook it until it is *al dente*. Drain the orzo and divide it between four deep plates. Ladle the mussels and sauce over each serving.

Gemelli with Sun-Dried Tomatoes, Rosemary and Thyme

Serves 8 as an appetizer
Working time: about 25 minutes
Total time: about 30 minutes

Calories **175**
Protein **5g**
Cholesterol **5mg**
Total fat **6g**
Saturated fat **1g**
Sodium **250mg**

250 g	gemelli (or short tubular pasta)	8 oz
60 g	sun-dried tomatoes packed in oil, drained and thinly sliced	2 oz
4	small leeks, trimmed, cleaned and cut into 2 cm (¾ inch) slices	4
2	shallots, finely chopped	2
1 tsp	fresh rosemary, or ¼ tsp dried rosemary	1 tsp
1 ½ tbsp	fresh lemon juice	1 ½ tbsp
2 tbsp	virgin olive oil	2 tbsp
½ tsp	salt	½ tsp
	freshly ground black pepper	
1 tsp	fresh thyme, or ¼ tsp dried thyme	1 tsp
4 tbsp	dry white wine	4 tbsp
4 tbsp	freshly grated Parmesan cheese	4 tbsp

Precook the gemelli in 3 litres (5 pints) of unsalted boiling water for 2 minutes — the pasta will be underdone. Drain it and put it in a large fireproof casserole. Stir in the tomatoes, ¼ litre (8 fl oz) of water, 45 g (1 ½ oz) of the white part of the leeks, the shallots, rosemary, lemon juice, 1 tablespoon of the oil, ¼ teaspoon of the salt and some pepper. Cover the casserole and cook the mixture over low heat, stirring occasionally, until all the liquid has been absorbed — about 8 minutes.

Meanwhile, in a large, heavy frying pan, heat the remaining tablespoon of oil over medium heat. Add the remaining leek slices, the remaining ¼ teaspoon of salt, some pepper and the thyme. Cook the mixture for 3 minutes, stirring from time to time. Raise the heat to high and cook the mixture for 1 minute more, then pour in the wine. Cook until the liquid has evaporated — about 4 minutes.

Add the leek mixture to the casserole, then stir in the cheese. To infuse the pasta with the flavours of the herbs and sun-dried tomatoes, cover the casserole and let it stand for 5 minutes before serving it.

EDITOR'S NOTE: *Two tablespoons of the oil from the sun-dried tomatoes may be substituted for the olive oil called for here.*

Vermicelli with Tomatoes and Clams

BEFORE STEAMING THE CLAMS, DISCARD ANY THAT
FAIL TO CLOSE WHEN THEY ARE TAPPED.

Serves 4
Working (and total) time: about 1 hour

Calories **455**
Protein **24g**
Cholesterol **55mg**
Total fat **11g**
Saturated fat **3g**
Sodium **150mg**

250 g	vermicelli or thin spaghetti	8 oz
36	small clams, the shells scrubbed	36
6 tbsp	red wine	6 tbsp
5	parsley sprigs	5
6	garlic cloves, finely chopped	6
1½ tbsp	virgin olive oil	1½ tbsp
1	small carrot, peeled and thinly sliced	1
1	onion, finely chopped	1
2 kg	ripe tomatoes, skinned, seeded and chopped, or 1.3 kg (48 oz) canned whole tomatoes, drained and chopped	4 lb
2 tsp	finely chopped fresh oregano, or 1 tsp dried oregano	2 tsp
1½ tsp	finely chopped fresh thyme, or ½ tsp dried thyme	1½ tsp
	freshly ground black pepper	
15 g	unsalted butter	½ oz

In a large pan, combine the clams, wine, parsley and half of the garlic. Cover the pan tightly and steam the clams over medium-high heat for 5 minutes. Transfer to a bowl any clams that have opened. Re-cover the

pan and steam the remaining clams for about 3 minutes more. Again, transfer the opened clams to the bowl; discard any clams that are still closed. Strain the wine mixture remaining in the pan through a very fine sieve and reserve 6 tablespoons of it for the sauce. When the clams are cool enough to handle, remove them from their shells and reserve them along with any liquid remaining in the bowl.

To make the sauce, pour the oil into a heavy-bottomed saucepan over medium heat. Add the carrot and onion, and sauté them until the onion is translucent — about 5 minutes. Add the remaining garlic and cook the mixture for 3 minutes more. Stir in the tomatoes, oregano and thyme. Reduce the heat to low and continue cooking, stirring often, until the sauce is quite thick — about 15 minutes. Then add the clams to the sauce, along with their liquid and the reserved wine mixture. Stir in a generous amount of black pepper.

About 5 minutes after adding the tomatoes to the sauce, put the vermicelli into 3 litres (5 pints) of boiling water with 1½ teaspoons of salt. Start testing the vermicelli after 6 minutes and cook it until it is *al dente*.

Drain the vermicelli and return it to the cooking pan; add the butter and toss well to coat the pasta. Pour the clam sauce over the pasta and serve at once.

Ditalini Gratin with Chili Pepper

IN THIS DISH, PASTA AND SAUCE ARE COOKED TOGETHER, WITH THE STARCH IN THE PASTA SERVING AS THE THICKENING AGENT FOR THE SAUCE.

Serves 6 as a side dish
Working time: about 25 minutes
Total time: about 30 minutes

Calories **225**
Protein **10g**
Cholesterol **10mg**
Total fat **4g**
Saturated fat **3g**
Sodium **185mg**

250 g	ditalini (or other small, tubular pasta)	8 oz
750 g	ripe tomatoes, skinned, seeded and chopped, or 400 g (14 oz) canned whole tomatoes, drained and chopped	1½ lb
1	onion, chopped	1
¼ litre	semi-skimmed milk	8 fl oz
1	hot green chili pepper, seeded, deribbed and finely chopped (caution, page 33)	1
1	garlic clove, finely chopped	1
¼ tsp	ground cumin	¼ tsp
¼ tsp	salt	¼ tsp
	freshly ground black pepper	
60 g	Cheddar cheese, finely diced	2 oz

Put the tomatoes, onion and milk in a large, heavy sauté pan and bring the mixture to the boil. Add the ditalini, chili pepper, garlic, cumin, salt and a liberal grinding of black pepper. Stir to mix thoroughly, then cover the pan and reduce the heat to medium. Simmer the mixture for 2 minutes, stirring from time to time to keep the pasta from sticking to the bottom. Preheat the grill.

Pour into the pan just enough water to cover the ditalini. Cook the pasta, removing the lid frequently to stir the mixture and keep it covered with liquid, until the pasta is just tender and a creamy sauce has formed — about 7 minutes.

Transfer the contents of the pan to a fireproof gratin dish. Sprinkle the cheese over the top and grill the pasta until the cheese is melted — 2 to 3 minutes. Serve the dish immediately.

Fettuccine with Grilled Aubergine

Serves 4
Working time: about 30 minutes
Total time: about 40 minutes

Calories **355**
Protein **9g**
Cholesterol **0mg**
Total fat **13g**
Saturated fat **1g**
Sodium **235mg**

250 g	fettuccine (or other narrow ribbon pasta)	8 oz
500 g	aubergines, cut lengthwise into 2.5 cm (1 inch) slices	1 lb
2½ tbsp	virgin olive oil	2½ tbsp
1	large, ripe tomato, skinned and seeded	1
50 g	oil-packed sun-dried tomatoes, drained and thinly sliced	1¾ oz
1	shallot, finely chopped	1
1	garlic clove, finely chopped	1
1 tbsp	red wine vinegar	1 tbsp
	freshly ground black pepper	
4 tbsp	chopped fresh basil	4 tbsp

Preheat the grill. Brush both sides of the aubergine slices with 1½ tablespoons of the oil. Cut each aubergine slice into cubes. Put the aubergine cubes on a baking sheet in a single layer, then grill them until they are well browned on one side. Turn the pieces over and grill once more until brown. Turn off the grill, but leave the aubergine underneath to keep it warm.

Cook the fettuccine in 3 litres (5 pints) of boiling water with 1½ teaspoons of salt; start testing the pasta after 10 minutes and cook it until it is *al dente*.

Purée the fresh tomato in a food processor or blender. Put the tomato purée in a small saucepan along with the sun-dried tomatoes, shallot, garlic, vinegar,

the remaining tablespoon of oil and a generous grinding of pepper. Place the pan over low heat, bring the mixture to a simmer, and cook it for 2 minutes. Remove the pan from the heat and stir in the basil.

When the pasta finishes cooking, drain it and transfer it to a large serving bowl. Add the warm aubergine cubes and the sauce, toss well, and serve at once.

EDITOR'S NOTE: *Two and a half tablespoons of the oil in which the sun-dried tomatoes are packed may be substituted for the virgin olive oil called for here.*

Vermicelli with Prawns and Fennel

Serves 6
Working time: about 35 minutes
Total time: about 45 minutes

Calories **365**
Protein **17g**
Cholesterol **85mg**
Total fat **12g**
Saturated fat **4g**
Sodium **225mg**

350 g	vermicelli (or other thin spaghetti)	12 oz
325 g	raw Mediterranean prawns, peeled, deveined and halved lengthwise	11 oz
½ tsp	fennel seeds (optional), crushed with a mortar and pestle	½ tsp
4	shallots, thinly sliced	4
2	garlic cloves, very finely chopped	2
	freshly ground black pepper	
2 tbsp	virgin olive oil	2 tbsp
1	lemon, cut in half	1
2	fennel bulbs (about 325 g/11 oz), stalks and green feathery tops reserved for another use, bulbs very thinly sliced	2
45 g	unsalted butter	1½ oz
4 tbsp	dry breadcrumbs	4 tbsp

Put the prawns, fennel seeds if you are using them, shallot and garlic in a bowl. Grind in plenty of black pepper, then add 1 tablespoon of the oil and mix well. Squeeze the juice of one lemon half into the bowl, mix well again, and set the bowl aside. Put the fennel slices in a separate small bowl and squeeze the juice of the remaining lemon half over them.

Heat the remaining tablespoon of oil in a large frying pan over high heat. When the oil is hot, add the fennel slices and sauté them, stirring constantly, for 5 minutes. Add the prawn mixture and cook just until the prawns turn pink — about 2 minutes. Transfer the contents of the pan to a serving bowl and set the bowl aside in a warm place.

Return the pan to the stove and reduce the heat to low. Melt the butter in the pan. Add the breadcrumbs and cook them, stirring often, until they are crisp and golden-brown — about 4 minutes.

While the breadcrumbs are browning, add the vermicelli to 3 litres (5 pints) of boiling water with 1½ teaspoons of salt. Cook the pasta until it is *al dente* — about 4 minutes. Drain the pasta, add it to the prawn-and-fennel mixture, and toss well. Scatter the breadcrumbs over the pasta and serve immediately.

Cannelloni Stuffed with Turkey, Kale and Cheese

Serves 6
Working time: about 30 minutes
Total time: about 2 hours

Calories **450**
Protein **38g**
Cholesterol **70mg**
Total fat **12g**
Saturated fat **7g**
Sodium **470mg**

12	cannelloni tubes (about 250 g/8 oz)	12
500 g	turkey breast meat, cut into 2.5 cm (1 inch) cubes	1 lb
1	small onion, finely chopped	1
½ tsp	fresh thyme, or ¼ tsp dried thyme	½ tsp
4 tbsp	dry vermouth	4 tbsp
½ litre	unsalted chicken stock	16 fl oz
250 g	low-fat ricotta cheese	8 oz
250 g	low-fat cottage cheese	8 oz
6 tbsp	freshly grated Parmesan cheese	6 tbsp
250 g	kale, cooked, thoroughly drained and finely chopped	8 oz
	freshly ground black pepper	
	grated nutmeg	
30 g	unsalted butter	1 oz
4 tbsp	plain flour	4 tbsp
½ litre	skimmed milk	16 fl oz

To begin making the stuffing, combine the turkey cubes, onion, thyme and vermouth in a bowl. Allow the cubes to marinate for at least 30 minutes.

Strain the marinade into a large, non-reactive frying pan over medium heat. Pour in the stock and bring the liquid to a simmer. Add the turkey cubes and poach them until they are no longer pink at the centre — about 4 minutes.

With a slotted spoon, transfer the cubes to a food processor, reserving their poaching liquid. Operate the machine in short bursts until the cubes are finely chopped. Add the ricotta, the cottage cheese, 4 tablespoons of the Parmesan and the kale, and mix. Season the mixture with pepper and nutmeg, and set it aside.

To prepare the sauce, melt the butter in a large saucepan over medium heat. Gradually whisk in the flour to make a paste and cook for 2 minutes. Add the reserved poaching liquid and bring the mixture to the boil, whisking constantly to prevent lumps from form-

ing. Pour in the milk and return the liquid to the boil, whisking frequently. Reduce the heat to low and let the sauce simmer gently for about 15 minutes while you prepare the cannelloni.

Add the tubes to 4 litres (7 pints) of boiling water with 2 teaspoons of salt. Start testing the pasta after 15 minutes and cook it until it is *al dente*. When the cannelloni are done, transfer them to a bowl of cold water.

Preheat the oven to 200°C (400°F or Mark 6). Thoroughly drain the cannelloni tubes and stuff each one carefully with the turkey mixture.

Arrange the cannelloni in a single layer in a large bak-

ing dish. Ladle the sauce over the cannelloni and sprinkle the remaining 2 tablespoons of Parmesan cheese over the top. Cover the dish with aluminium foil and bake it until the sauce bubbles and the pasta is heated through — about 30 minutes. Remove the foil from the dish and brown the cannelloni under the grill for about 5 minutes. Serve immediately.

EDITOR'S NOTE: *To allow for cannelloni tubes that may tear during cooking or while being stuffed, add one or two extra tubes to the boiling water. The cannelloni may be assembled in advance and refrigerated for up to 24 hours before the sauce and Parmesan cheese are added and the dish is baked.*

Lasagnette with Lobster, Spring Greens and Brown Butter

Serves 2
Working time: about 30 minutes
Total time: about 1 hour

Calories **430**
Protein **25g**
Cholesterol **105mg**
Total fat **15g**
Saturated fat **7g**
Sodium **425mg**

125 g	lasagnette (or other curly-edged ribbon pasta)	4 oz
1	live lobster (about 600 g/1 ¼ lb)	1
1	lemon or lime, cut in half	1
250 g	spring greens, washed, stemmed and cut into 1 cm (½ inch) strips	8 oz
30 g	unsalted butter	1 oz
	freshly ground black pepper	

Pour enough water into a large pot to fill it to a depth of about 2.5 cm (1 inch). Bring the water to the boil and add the lobster. Cover the pot tightly and steam the lobster until it turns a bright reddish orange — about 10 minutes. Remove the lobster from the pot and set it on a dish to catch the juices; do not discard the cooking liquid. Pour 2 litres (3½ pints) of water into the pot and bring the liquid to the boil.

Holding the lobster over the dish, remove the tail by twisting it away from the body. Twist the claws off the body, then crack the shell of the tail and claws. Remove the meat and slice it thinly. Add the shells and lobster juices to the pot with the boiling liquid. Allow the shells to boil for 10 minutes. With a slotted spoon, remove the shells and discard them. Squeeze the juice of one of the lemon or lime halves into the liquid. Add the lasagnette and cover the pot. When the liquid returns to the boil, remove the lid. Start testing the pasta after 11 minutes and cook it until it is *al dente*.

While the pasta is cooking, transfer 6 tablespoons of the cooking liquid to a large, heavy sauté pan and bring it to a simmer. Add the spring greens and cook

them, stirring occasionally, until all of the liquid has evaporated and the greens are completely wilted. Melt the butter in a small, heavy-bottomed saucepan over medium heat and cook it just until it turns nut brown; watch the butter carefully after it stops bubbling lest it burn. Scatter the lobster meat over the spring greens in the pan. Squeeze the juice of the remaining lemon or lime half over the lobster.

When the pasta finishes cooking, drain it and add it to the pan. Add some pepper, pour the butter over the pasta, and toss well. Serve immediately.

Linguine and Chilied Prawns

Serves 4
Working time: about 20 minutes
Total time: about 1 hour

Calories **495**
Protein **23g**
Cholesterol **135mg**
Total fat **20g**
Saturated fat **6g**
Sodium **390mg**

250 g	linguine (or spaghetti)	8 oz
45 g	unsalted butter	1½ oz
1	onion, finely chopped	1
35 cl	light beer	12 fl oz
1	bay leaf	1
2 tbsp	safflower oil	2 tbsp
500 g	large fresh prawns, peeled and deveined, the shells reserved	1 lb
1	garlic clove, finely chopped	1
1 tbsp	chili powder	1 tbsp
¼ tsp	salt	¼ tsp
	freshly ground black pepper	
⅓	avocado, peeled and thinly sliced	⅓

To make the sauce, melt the butter in a saucepan over medium-high heat. Add the onion and cook it until it is translucent — about 2 minutes. Add the beer, bay leaf and reserved prawn shells, and bring the liquid to a simmer. Reduce the heat to low, cover the pan, and simmer the mixture for 20 minutes.

Add the linguine to 3 litres (5 pints) of boiling water with 1½ teaspoons of salt. After 8 minutes, drain the pasta and set it aside; it will be slightly underdone.

Strain the prawn-shell liquid, discarding the solids, and return the liquid to the pan; there will be a little more than ¼ litre (8 fl oz). Add the reserved linguine to the liquid and simmer it, covered, until it is *al dente* — about 4 minutes.

While the pasta finishes cooking, pour the oil into a large, heavy frying pan over medium-high heat. Add the prawns and sauté them, stirring occasionally, until they are firm and opaque — 1 to 2 minutes. Stir in the garlic and cook for 30 seconds more. Season the prawns with the chili powder, the ¼ teapoon of salt and some pepper.

Add the avocado to the linguine and toss. Transfer the mixture to a platter, arrange the prawns on top of the pasta, and serve hot.

Linguine and Chicken in Parsley Sauce

Serves 4
Working time: about 25 minutes
Total time: about 30 minutes

Calories **400**
Protein **23g**
Cholesterol **50mg**
Total fat **13g**
Saturated fat **5g**
Sodium **305mg**

250 g	linguine (or spaghetti)	8 oz
1 tbsp	safflower oil	1 tbsp
1	lemon, rind only, finely julienned	1
1 tsp	finely chopped fresh ginger root	1 tsp
1 tsp	sugar	1 tsp
¼ tsp	salt	¼ tsp
¼ litre	unsalted chicken stock	8 fl oz
30 g	unsalted butter	1 oz
250 g	skinned and boned chicken breasts, cut into 2 cm (¾ inch) cubes	8 oz
2	shallots, finely chopped	2
2	bunches of parsley, stemmed (about 90 g/3 oz)	2

Cook the oil and lemon rind in a saucepan over medium heat for 4 minutes. Stir in the ginger, sugar and ⅛ teaspoon of the salt, and cook the mixture for 3 minutes more, stirring frequently. Pour in the stock and bring the mixture to the boil; cook it until only about 12.5 cl (4 fl oz) of liquid remains — 5 to 7 minutes.

Cook the linguine in 3 litres (5 pints) of boiling water with 1½ teaspoons of salt. Start testing the pasta after 10 minutes and cook it until it is *al dente*.

While the pasta is cooking, melt 15 g (½ oz) of the butter in a large, heavy frying pan over medium-high heat. Add the chicken cubes and shallots; sauté them, stirring frequently, until the cubes are lightly browned — about 3 minutes. Stir in the lemon rind mixture and cook for 1 minute more. Add the parsley and cook, stirring, for an additional 3 minutes.

Drain the pasta and transfer it to a casserole. Stir the remaining butter into the sauce and combine the sauce with the pasta. Cover the casserole and let the dish stand for 5 minutes, stirring once, to meld the flavours.

Spirals with Liver, Onions and Sugar Snap Peas

Serves 4
Working (and total) time: about 35 minutes

Calories **375**	250 g	spirals (or other short pasta)	8 oz
Protein **15g**	2 tbsp	virgin olive oil	2 tbsp
Cholesterol **130mg**			
Total fat **12g**	125 g	chicken livers, trimmed and cut into 1 cm (½ inch) pieces	4 oz
Saturated fat **3g**			
Sodium **265mg**	¼ tsp	salt	¼ tsp
	2	onions, thinly sliced	2
	4 tbsp	cider vinegar	4 tbsp
	15 g	unsalted butter	½ oz
	250 g	small sugar snap peas or mange-tout, trimmed and strings removed	8 oz
		freshly ground black pepper	

Heat 1 tablespoon of the oil in a large, non-stick or heavy frying pan over medium-high heat. Sauté the chicken liver pieces, stirring constantly, until they turn brown — 30 to 45 seconds. Sprinkle the liver pieces with ⅛ teaspoon of the salt, remove them from the pan and set them aside.

Return the pan to the heat without washing it and add the remaining tablespoon of oil. Add the onions and vinegar, and stir to deglaze the pan. Cook, stirring frequently, until the onions are golden-brown — about 15 minutes.

Meanwhile, cook the pasta in 3 litres (5 pints) of boiling water with 1½ teaspoons of salt. Begin testing the pasta after 8 minutes and cook it until it is *al dente*.

While the pasta is cooking, melt the butter in a frying pan over medium heat. Add the peas and cook them until they are tender — about 7 minutes. Sprinkle the peas with the remaining ⅛ teaspoon of salt and some pepper. Drain the pasta and add it to the pan containing the onions. Add the reserved liver pieces and peas, toss thoroughly, and serve immediately.

Spaghetti with Smoked Salmon and Watercress

Serves 4
Working (and total) time: about 15 minutes

Calories **245**			
Protein **10g**	250 g	spaghetti	8 oz
Cholesterol **5mg**	1½ tsp	virgin olive oil	1½ tsp
Total fat **3g**	1	garlic clove, finely chopped	1
Saturated fat **0g**	60 g	smoked salmon, julienned	2 oz
Sodium **215mg**	1	bunch watercress, washed and stemmed	1
		freshly ground black pepper	

Cook the spaghetti in 3 litres (5 pints) of boiling water with 1½ teaspoons of salt. Start testing the pasta after 8 minutes and cook it until it is *al dente*.

Just before the spaghetti finishes cooking, heat the oil in a large frying pan over medium heat. Cook the garlic in the oil for 30 seconds, stirring constantly. Add the salmon, watercress and pepper, and cook for 30 seconds more before removing the pan from the heat.

Drain the spaghetti and add it to the pan. Toss the spaghetti to distribute the sauce and serve at once.

Farfalle in Red Pepper Sauce with Broccoli

Serves 4
Working time: about 15 minutes
Total time: about 25 minutes

Calories **285**
Protein **11g**
Cholesterol **5mg**
Total fat **6g**
Saturated fat **2g**
Sodium **350mg**

250 g	farfalle (or other fancy-shaped pasta)	8 oz
1 tbsp	virgin olive oil	1 tbsp
1	garlic clove, finely chopped	1
2	sweet red peppers, seeded, deribbed and coarsely chopped	2
¼ tsp	salt	¼ tsp
¼ litre	unsalted chicken stock	8 fl oz
75 g	broccoli florets, blanched for 2 minutes and refreshed under cold running water	2½ oz
1 tbsp	chopped fresh basil, or 1 tsp dried basil	1 tbsp
½ tbsp	chopped fresh oregano, or ½ tsp dried oregano	½ tbsp
	freshly ground black pepper	
4 tbsp	freshly grated Parmesan cheese	4 tbsp

Heat the oil in a large, heavy frying pan over medium heat. Add the garlic and cook it for 30 seconds, stirring constantly. Add the red peppers, salt and stock. Simmer until only 6 tablespoons of liquid remain — 7 to 8 minutes. Meanwhile, cook the farfalle in 3 litres (5 pints) of boiling water with 1½ teaspoons of salt. Start testing the pasta after 8 minutes and cook it until it is *al dente*. Drain the pasta and transfer it to a bowl.

Purée the red pepper mixture in a blender or food processor. Strain it through a sieve back into the pan. Stir in the broccoli, basil, oregano, pepper and cheese. Simmer until the broccoli is heated through — 2 to 3 minutes. Toss the farfalle with the sauce and serve.

Pasta Shells and Scallops

Serves 6
Working (and total) time: about 25 minutes

Calories **300**
Protein **18g**
Cholesterol **40mg**
Total fat **9g**
Saturated fat **4g**
Sodium **460mg**

250 g	medium pasta shells	8 oz
1 tbsp	safflower oil	1 tbsp
1	small onion, finely chopped	1
2 tbsp	flour	2 tbsp
35 cl	unsalted chicken or fish stock	12 fl oz
4 tbsp	double cream	4 tbsp
⅛ tsp	grated nutmeg	⅛ tsp
¼ tsp	salt	¼ tsp
¼ tsp	white pepper	¼ tsp
350 g	scallops, connective muscle at their sides removed, as necessary	12 oz
4 tbsp	fresh breadcrumbs	4 tbsp
60 g	Parmesan cheese, freshly grated	2 oz
¼ tsp	paprika	¼ tsp
	parsley sprigs for garnish	

Add the pasta shells to 3 litres (5 pints) of boiling water with 1½ teaspoons of salt. Start testing the pasta after 8 minutes and cook it until it is *al dente*.

Meanwhile, to prepare the sauce, pour the oil into a shallow fireproof casserole over medium heat. Add the onion and sauté it until it turns translucent — about 3 minutes. Stir in the flour and continue to cook, stirring constantly, for 2 minutes. Remove the casserole from the heat. Slowly whisk in the stock and cream, stirring the mixture until it is smooth. Add the nutmeg, salt and pepper, and stir. Preheat the grill.

Drain the pasta and add it, along with the scallops, to the sauce. Return the casserole to the heat and bring the sauce to a simmer. Cover the casserole and simmer gently until the scallops become opaque — 2 to 3 minutes.

To prepare the dish for the table, wipe any sauce from the visible inside walls of the casserole. Then top the dish with the breadcrumbs, cheese and paprika and grill it until the topping is golden — about 2 minutes. Garnish with the parsley sprigs and serve hot.

Rigatoni with Red Potatoes and Radicchio

Serves 6 as an appetizer
Working (and total) time: about 45 minutes

Calories **275**
Protein **7g**
Cholesterol **0mg**
Total fat **10g**
Saturated fat **1g**
Sodium **100mg**

250 g	rigatoni (or medium shells)	8 oz
3	unpeeled red potatoes (about 250 g/8 oz), each cut into 8 pieces	3
4 tbsp	virgin olive oil	4 tbsp
250 g	spinach, washed, stemmed, and squeezed into a ball to remove excess water	8 oz
2	garlic cloves, finely chopped	2
125 g	radicchio, torn into 4 cm (1½ inch) pieces	4 oz
2 tbsp	Dijon mustard	2 tbsp
2 tbsp	red wine vinegar	2 tbsp
4 tbsp	chopped fresh basil	4 tbsp
2	bunches spring onions, trimmed and cut into 2.5 cm (1 inch) pieces	2
	freshly ground black pepper	

In a large, covered pan, bring 3 litres (5 pints) of water and 1½ teaspoons of salt to the boil; add the rigatoni to the boiling water. Start testing the pasta after 13 minutes and cook it until it is *al dente*.

While the pasta is cooking, pour enough water into a saucepan to fill it about 2.5 cm (1 inch) deep. Add ½ teaspoon of salt and set a vegetable steamer in the bottom of the pan. Bring the water to the boil. Add the potatoes, cover the pan, and steam the potatoes until they are tender when pierced with the tip of a thin knife — about 8 minutes. Transfer the potatoes to a large bowl.

When the pasta is cooked, drain it and transfer it to the bowl with the potatoes. Pour in 1 tablespoon of the oil and toss well to coat the pasta and the potatoes.

Heat another tablespoon of the oil in a large, heavy frying pan over medium-high heat. When it is hot, add the spinach and garlic, and sauté them for 30 seconds, stirring constantly. Add the radicchio and cook until the spinach has wilted — about 30 seconds more. Scrape the contents of the pan into the bowl containing the pasta and the potatoes.

In a small bowl, whisk together the mustard and vinegar. Whisk in the remaining oil, then pour over the pasta. Add the basil, spring onions and some pepper to the bowl, toss well to combine, and serve.

EDITOR'S NOTE: *This dish may be served warm, at room temperature, or chilled.*

Capelli d'Angelo with Tomatoes, Black Olives and Garlic

Serves 6 as an appetizer
Working time: about 20 minutes
Total time: about 1 hour

Calories **190**
Protein **6g**
Cholesterol **0mg**
Total fat **4g**
Saturated fat **0g**
Sodium **190mg**

250 g	capelli d'angelo (or vermicelli)	8 oz
3	large, ripe tomatoes, skinned, seeded and chopped	3
4	garlic cloves, finely chopped	4
5	black olives, stoned and finely chopped	5
1	small hot chili pepper, seeded, deribbed and finely chopped (caution, page 33)	1
1 tbsp	virgin olive oil	1 tbsp
1	lime, juice only	1
1 tbsp	chopped fresh coriander	1 tbsp
⅛ tsp	salt	⅛ tsp
	freshly ground black pepper	

Put the chopped tomatoes in a strainer set over a large bowl; place the bowl in the refrigerator and let the tomatoes drain for at least 30 minutes.

Put 3 litres (5 pints) of water on to boil with 1½ teaspoons of salt. In a separate bowl, combine the garlic, olives, chili pepper, oil, lime juice, coriander, salt and pepper. Refrigerate the mixture.

Drop the capelli d'angelo into the boiling water. Begin testing them after 3 minutes and continue to cook until they are *al dente*.

While the pasta is cooking, combine the garlic mixture with the drained tomatoes; discard the juice. Drain the pasta, transfer it to a serving bowl and toss it immediately with the sauce.

Cavatappi with Spinach and Ham

Serves 4
Working time: about 25 minutes
Total time: about 35 minutes

Calories **330**
Protein **13g**
Cholesterol **35mg**
Total fat **11g**
Saturated fat **5g**
Sodium **360mg**

250 g	cavatappi (or other short, tubular pasta)	8 oz
10 g	unsalted butter	⅓ oz
1	small onion, finely chopped	1
2	garlic cloves, finely chopped	2
½ litre	unsalted chicken stock	16 fl oz
4 tbsp	dry vermouth	4 tbsp
4 tbsp	double cream	4 tbsp
1	bay leaf	1
	grated nutmeg	
	freshly ground black pepper	
60 g	lean ham, julienned	2 oz
500 g	fresh spinach, washed and stemmed	1 lb

Melt the butter in a large non-reactive frying pan over medium-high heat. Add the onion and garlic, and sauté them until they turn translucent — about 5 minutes. Add the stock, vermouth, cream, bay leaf, a little nutmeg and some pepper, and cook the mixture until it is reduced to about ¼ litre (8 fl oz) — 10 to 15 minutes.

While the stock mixture is reducing, add the pasta to 3 litres (5 pints) of boiling water with 1½ teaspoons of salt. Start testing the pasta after 10 minutes and cook it until it is *al dente*.

About 3 minutes before the pasta finishes cooking, remove the bay leaf from the mixture in the pan and discard it. Stir in the ham and spinach, then cover the pan and steam the spinach for 3 minutes. Remove the cover and stir the mixture until the spinach is completely wilted — about 30 seconds. Turn off the heat.

Drain the pasta and immediately stir it into the spinach and ham mixture. Allow the pasta mixture to stand for 1 minute. Stir it again just before serving.

Noodles, Cabbage and Caraway

Serves 6 as a side dish
Working time: about 15 minutes
Total time: about 50 minutes

Calories **165**
Protein **5g**
Cholesterol **30mg**
Total fat **4g**
Saturated fat **2g**
Sodium **155mg**

175 g	wide or extra-wide egg noodles	6 oz
2	onions, sliced	2
6 tbsp	cider vinegar	6 tbsp
1½ tbsp	unsalted butter	1½ tbsp
¾ tsp	caraway seeds	¾ tsp
¼ tsp	salt	¼ tsp
350 g	cabbage, cored and cut into 2.5 cm (1 inch) strips	12 oz
1 tbsp	paprika, preferably Hungarian	1 tbsp
1 tsp	dark brown sugar	1 tsp
	freshly ground black pepper	

Pour 17.5 cl (6 fl oz) of water into a large pan. Add the onions, vinegar, butter, caraway seeds and salt, and bring the mixture to the boil. Cook, stirring frequently, for 5 minutes. Reduce the heat to medium-low, then stir in the cabbage, paprika and brown sugar. Cover the pan and cook for 35 minutes, removing the lid three times to stir. Add water, if necessary, to ensure that the liquid in the pan remains about 1 cm (½ inch) deep.

Approximately 5 minutes before the cabbage finishes cooking, drop the noodles into 2 litres (3½ pints) of boiling water with 1 teaspoon of salt and cook them for 5 minutes. The noodles will be undercooked. Drain them and add them to the cabbage mixture along with some pepper. Cook over medium-low heat, stirring occasionally, until all the liquid has evaporated and the noodles are *al dente* — 5 to 7 minutes.

Lasagnette with Chicken, Mango and Raisins

Serves 4
Working time: about 20 minutes
Total time: about 1 hour

Calories **465**
Protein **32g**
Cholesterol **90mg**
Total fat **8g**
Saturated fat **2g**
Sodium **200mg**

250 g	narrow lasagnette	8 oz
6	chicken drumsticks, skinned and boned, the meat cut into 2.5 cm (1 inch) pieces	6
⅛ tsp	cayenne pepper	⅛ tsp
¼ tsp each	ground cloves, cinnamon, cardamom and cumin	¼ tsp each
1 tsp	ground turmeric	1 tsp
1 tbsp	virgin olive oil	1 tbsp
1	large onion, chopped finely	1
4	garlic cloves, crushed	4
¼ tsp	salt	¼ tsp
35 cl	unsalted chicken stock	12 fl oz
1	mango, peeled, the flesh cut into neat cubes	1
30 g	raisins	1 oz
2 tbsp	finely chopped parsley	2 tbsp

Put the chicken pieces into a mixing bowl, sprinkle with the spices and toss well to coat evenly. Cover the bowl and let it stand at room temperature for at least 30 minutes.

Heat the oil in a large, heavy-bottomed sauté pan over medium heat, tilting the pan to coat it evenly. Add the onion and garlic and sauté them, stirring constantly, until the onion is translucent — about 3 minutes. Sprinkle the salt over the chicken, then add the pieces to the pan. Sauté, stirring frequently, for about 5 minutes, until the chicken is very lightly browned. Pour the stock into the pan and bring to the boil. Add the mango and raisins. Reduce the heat, partially cover the pan and simmer gently for 20 minutes.

Meanwhile, cook the lasagnette in 3 litres (5 pints) of boiling water with 1½ teaspoons of salt. Start testing after 10 minutes and cook until they are *al dente*.

Drain the pasta well, then put it into a large heated serving bowl. Add the chicken mixture and the parsley. Toss gently together and serve immediately.

EDITOR'S NOTE: *Lemon wedges and a bowl of thinly sliced onion rings make a good accompaniment to this pasta dish.*

Spinach Shell Salad with Chunks of Chicken

Serves 4
Working (and total) time: about 40 minutes

Calories **320**
Protein **22g**
Cholesterol **35mg**
Total fat **3g**
Saturated fat **1g**
Sodium **270mg**

250 g	medium spinach shells	8 oz
250 g	chicken breasts, skinned and boned, cut into pieces about 2.5 cm (1 inch) square	8 oz
¼ tsp	salt	¼ tsp
	freshly ground black pepper	
2	large shallots, thinly sliced	2
½ tsp	ground cinnamon	½ tsp
750 g	ripe tomatoes, skinned, seeded and chopped	1½ lb
1	orange, rind only, cut into thin strips	1

Arrange the chicken pieces in a single layer in a deep, heatproof dish about 25 cm (10 inches) in diameter. Sprinkle the chicken with the salt and pepper. Scatter the shallot slices evenly over the chicken and top them with the cinnamon and tomatoes. Strew the orange rind over all. Cover the dish tightly with foil.

Pour enough water into a saucepan approximately 20 cm (8 inches) in diameter to fill it about one third full. Bring the water to a rolling boil. Set the covered dish on top of the saucepan like a lid and cook the chicken over the boiling water. After 5 minutes, test the chicken: if the meat is still pink at the centre, cover the dish again and continue to steam the chicken until all trace of pink has disappeared and the meat feels firm but springy to the touch. Remove the dish from the saucepan and uncover it.

While the chicken is cooking, add the shells to 3 litres (5 pints) of boiling water with 1½ teaspoons of salt. Start testing the shells after 12 minutes and cook them until they are *al dente*.

Drain the shells and transfer them to a heated bowl. Add the chicken-and-tomato sauce and toss it with the shells. Serve hot or at room temperature.

Macaroni Salad

Serves 6
Working (and total) time: about 30 minutes

Calories **240**
Protein **17g**
Cholesterol **5mg**
Total fat **8g**
Saturated fat **2g**
Sodium **400mg**

250 g	elbow macaroni	8 oz
1 tbsp	safflower oil	1 tbsp
1	clove garlic, crushed	1
100 g	fresh shelled or frozen garden peas	3½ oz
100 g	fresh or frozen sweetcorn kernels	3½ oz
100 g	fine French beans, trimmed and cut into pea-size pieces	3½ oz
¼ tsp	salt	¼ tsp
	freshly ground black pepper	
1 tsp	finely chopped fresh thyme, or ½ tsp dried thyme	1 tsp
¼ litre	unsalted chicken stock	8 fl oz
1½ tbsp	white wine vinegar	1½ tbsp
1	small chili pepper, seeded, deribbed and finely chopped (caution page 33)	1
100 g	lean ham, chopped	3½ oz
1	large cos lettuce, trimmed and washed	1
Garnish		
1	large tomato, skinned, seeded and neatly chopped	1
2	large spring onions, trimmed and finely sliced	2
1 tbsp	finely chopped fresh basil, or ½ tbsp dried basil	1 tbsp

Cook the macaroni in 3 litres (5 pints) of boiling water with 1½ teaspoons of salt. Start testing after 8 minutes and cook until it is *al dente*. Drain the macaroni, and rinse it briefly under cold water. Drain the pasta again, then spread it out on a clean tea towel to remove any excess moisture.

Heat the oil in a large, heavy-bottomed sauté pan over medium heat. Add the garlic and cook for about 30 seconds. Add the peas, sweetcorn, beans, salt, pepper, thyme and stock. Bring the mixture to a simmer and cook gently until the liquid is reduced by two thirds, about 10 minutes. Allow to cool.

Meanwhile, pour the vinegar into a small bowl, add the chili pepper and leave to stand for 5 minutes to allow the vinegar to mellow the pepper's hotness.

Put the macaroni into a large mixing bowl, stir in the chili vinegar and the pea, sweetcorn, bean and stock mixture. Add the chopped ham and mix everything well together.

Line a large serving dish with cos lettuce leaves and spoon the macaroni mixture into the centre. Garnish the salad with the chopped tomato, spring onions and basil.

Egg Noodles with Carrots, Mange-Tout and Lamb

THIS DISH MAY BE SERVED WARM OR COLD.

Serves 4

Working (and total) time: about 40 minutes

Calories **500**
Protein **20g**
Cholesterol **85mg**
Total fat **23g**
Saturated fat **10g**
Sodium **295mg**

250 g	fine egg noodles	8 oz
2 tsp	honey	2 tsp
2 tbsp	lime juice	2 tbsp
1½ tsp	curry powder	1½ tsp
2 tbsp	virgin olive oil	2 tbsp
250 g	lean boneless lamb, cut into strips about 2.5 cm (1 inch) long and 5 mm (¼ inch) wide	8 oz
1	garlic clove, finely chopped	1
¼ tsp	salt	¼ tsp
4	spring onions, trimmed and thinly sliced, white and green parts kept separate	4
12.5 cl	unsalted chicken stock	4 fl oz
1	large carrot, peeled, halved lengthwise and sliced diagonally into very thin crescents	1
125 g	mange-tout, trimmed, strings removed, each pod sliced diagonally into thirds	4 oz

In a small dish, combine the honey, lime juice and curry powder; set the mixture aside. Add the noodles to 3 litres (5 pints) of boiling water with 1½ teaspoons of salt. Start testing the noodles after 5 minutes and cook them until they are *al dente*. Drain the noodles, transfer them to a large bowl, and toss them with 1 tablespoon of the oil.

Pour the remaining tablespoon of olive oil into a large, heavy frying pan over medium-high heat. When the oil is hot, add the lamb and cook it, stirring constantly, for about 30 seconds. Stir in the garlic, ⅛ teaspoon of the salt, the white part of the spring onions and the honey mixture. Cook for 30 seconds more, stirring constantly. Scrape the mixture into the bowl with the noodles and toss well. Do not wash the pan.

Return the pan to the stove over medium-high heat; pour in the stock, then add the carrot and the remaining ⅛ teaspoon of salt. Cook the mixture, scraping up any caramelized bits, for about 3 minutes. Add the mange-tout and cook for 1 minute more, stirring all the while. Transfer the mixture to the bowl with the noodles, add the spring onion greens, and mix thoroughly.

Wholewheat Spirals with Caviare Sauce

Serves 6
Working (and total) time: about 25 minutes

Calories **245**
Protein **12g**
Cholesterol **90mg**
Total fat **11g**
Saturated fat **3g**
Sodium **460mg**

250 g	wholewheat spirals (or other wholewheat pasta)	8 oz
1 tbsp	virgin olive oil	1 tbsp
1	large onion, finely chopped	1
17.5 cl	plain low-fat yogurt	6 fl oz
12.5 cl	soured cream	4 fl oz
100 g	lumpfish roe or caviare	3½ oz
2 tbsp	finely chopped parsley	2 tbsp
	freshly ground black pepper	
	watercress for garnish	

Cook the wholewheat spirals in 3 litres (5 pints) of boiling water. Start testing after 10 minutes and cook them until they are *al dente*.

Five minutes before the pasta is cooked, heat the oil in a heavy-bottomed saucepan, add the chopped onion and cook it very gently until it is translucent but still firm — about 3 minutes.

Stir in the yogurt and the soured cream. Heat the mixture gently until it is hot, but do not allow the sauce to boil. Stir in the lumpfish roe or caviare — reserving some for garnish — and the parsley and pepper.

Drain the pasta, pour on the sauce, and toss the pasta and sauce gently together. Turn the spirals on to a hot serving dish and garnish with the reserved roe or caviare and watercress. Serve immediately.

Terrine of Butternut Squash and Egg Noodles

Serves 12 as a dish
Working time: about 40 minutes
Total time: about 1 hour and 15 minutes

Calories **190**
Protein **6g**
Cholesterol **45mg**
Total fat **5g**
Saturated fat **2g**
Sodium **200mg**

300 g	wide egg noodles	10 oz
¾ tsp	salt	¾ tsp
½ tsp	ground cinnamon	½ tsp
½ tsp	ground coriander	½ tsp
1 tsp	ground allspice	1 tsp
	freshly ground black pepper	
1.25 kg	butternut squash or pumpkin, peeled, halved lengthwise and seeded, cut into 5 mm (¼ inch) slices	2½ lb
2 tbsp	safflower oil	2 tbsp
1	onion, finely chopped	1
1	egg and 3 egg whites, lightly beaten	1
15 g	unsalted butter	½ oz

Preheat the oven to 180°C (350°F or Mark 4). Combine the salt, spices and some pepper in a small bowl. Brush the squash slices with 1 tablespoon of the oil and arrange them in a single layer on a baking sheet. Sprinkle them with half the spice mixture and bake until softened — about 15 minutes. Leave the oven on.

While the squash cooks, bring 2 litres (3½ pints) of water with 1 teaspoon of salt to the boil. Pour the remaining tablespoon of oil into a frying pan over medium heat. Add the onion and some more pepper and cook, stirring frequently, until the onion is translucent — about 7 minutes. Meanwhile, add the noodles to the boiling water and cook them until they are almost *al dente* — about 7 minutes.

Drain the noodles and return them to their pan. Add the egg and egg whites to the noodles along with the remaining spice mixture. Add the butter, 4 tablespoons of water and the onion, and stir until the butter is melted.

Butter a 23 by 12.5 cm (9 by 5 inch) loaf pan. Line the bottom and sides of the pan with squash slices, covering all surfaces completely; reserve about one third of the slices for the top. Add the noodle mixture and press it down to make it compact. Arrange the reserved squash slices evenly over the top and cover them with a piece of greaseproof paper. Put a heavy, flat-bottomed object, such as a brick or a casserole, on top of the paper to weight the contents down, then bake the terrine for 35 minutes. Let the terrine stand for 10 minutes before unmoulding it.

To unmould the terrine, loosen it by running a knife around the inside of the pan, pressing it against the pan. Invert a serving dish over the pan, then turn both dish and pan over together. Carefully lift away the pan. Present the terrine whole or cut into serving slices; it is also good chilled.

Stellette with Smoked Salmon, Yogurt and Dill

Serves 6
Working (and total) time: about 25 minutes

Calories **200**
Protein **12g**
Cholesterol **15mg**
Total fat **1g**
Saturated fat **0g**
Sodium **400mg**

250 g	stellette (or other small pasta)	8 oz
2 tsp	Dijon mustard	2 tsp
2 tbsp	chopped fresh dill	2 tbsp
1 tbsp	lemon juice	1 tbsp
30 cl	plain low-fat yogurt	10 fl oz
	freshly ground black pepper	
150 g	smoked salmon, cut into long thin strips	5 oz
	cucumber slices	
Garnish		
2	limes, cut into wedges	2
	fresh dill	

Bring 3 litres (5 pints) of water containing 1½ teaspoons of salt to the boil and add the stellette to the water. Start testing the stellette after 2 minutes, then cook them until they are *al dente*. Drain them well. Rinse them briefly under cold running water and drain them once again. Then spread them out on a clean tea towel to remove any excess moisture.

In a large bowl, combine the mustard, chopped dill, lemon juice and plain yogurt. Add the stellette to the mixture and mix everything together. Season with freshly ground black pepper.

Mound the stellette on a large serving platter, and arrange the cucumber slices and the smoked salmon strips round the edge. Garnish with the lime wedges and fresh dill.

Afghan Noodles

Serves 6
Working time: about 35 minutes
Total time: about 45 minutes

Calories **350**
Protein **24g**
Cholesterol **45mg**
Total fat **12g**
Saturated fat **5g**
Sodium **325mg**

250 g	wide curly egg noodles	8 oz
¼ litre	low-fat yogurt, drained in a fine-meshed sieve or a muslin-lined sieve for 30 minutes	8 fl oz
4 tbsp	chopped fresh mint, or 2 tbsp dried mint	4 tbsp
2½ tsp	chili powder	2½ tsp
1 tbsp	fresh lemon juice	1 tbsp
1 tbsp	safflower oil	1 tbsp
1	onion, finely chopped	1
500 g	lean beef, minced	1 lb
½ tsp	salt	½ tsp
1	ripe tomato, skinned, seeded and chopped	1
15 g	unsalted butter	½ oz

To prepare the sauce, combine the drained yogurt with 3 tablespoons of the fresh mint or 1½ tablespoons of the dried mint, ½ teaspoon of the chili powder and the lemon juice.

Heat the oil in a large, heavy frying pan over medium-high heat. Add the onion and sauté it for 3 minutes. Add the beef, the remaining 2 teaspoons of chili powder and the salt, and cook the mixture for 6 minutes, stirring frequently. Stir in the tomato and cook for 2 minutes more.

Meanwhile, cook the egg noodles in 3 litres (5 pints) of boiling water with 1½ teaspoons of salt until they are *al dente* — about 9 minutes. Drain the noodles and return them to the pan. Add the butter and stir gently until it melts and the noodles are coated.

To serve, transfer the hot noodles to a warmed serving platter. Pour the sauce over the noodles in a ring 2.5 to 5 cm (1 to 2 inches) in from the edge of the noodles, then arrange the beef mixture in the centre of the ring. Sprinkle the remaining mint over the top of the assembly and serve immediately.

Egg Noodles with Poppy Seeds, Yogurt and Mushrooms

Serves 8 as a side dish
Working (and total) time: about 25 minutes

Calories **195**
Protein **6g**
Cholesterol **30mg**
Total fat **6g**
Saturated fat **2g**
Sodium **145mg**

250 g	medium egg noodles	8 oz
4 tbsp	soured cream	4 tbsp
12.5 cl	low-fat yogurt	4 fl oz
1 tbsp	poppy seeds	1 tbsp
⅛ to ¼ tsp	cayenne pepper	⅛ to ¼ tsp
2 tbsp	virgin olive oil	2 tbsp
250 g	mushrooms, wiped clean and thinly sliced	8 oz
1	onion, chopped	1
¼ tsp	salt	¼ tsp
12.5 cl	dry white wine	4 fl oz

In a small bowl, combine the soured cream, yogurt, poppy seeds, cayenne pepper and 1 tablespoon of the oil. In a large, covered pan, cook the egg noodles in 3 litres (5 pints) of boiling water with 1½ teaspoons of salt until they are *al dente* — about 9 minutes.

While the noodles are cooking, heat the remaining tablespoon of oil in a large, heavy frying pan over medium-high heat. Add the mushrooms and onion, and sprinkle them with the ¼ teaspoon of salt. Cook, stirring frequently, until the mushrooms and onion are browned all over — 5 to 7 minutes. Add the wine to the pan and continue cooking, stirring, until almost all of the liquid has been absorbed — about 3 minutes more.

When the noodles are done, drain them and add them to the pan. Add the yogurt and poppy seed mixture, toss well and serve.

Noodles with Asparagus, Mushrooms and Prosciutto

Serves 4
Working (and total) time: about 20 minutes

Calories **445**		
Protein **17g**		
Cholesterol **65mg**		
Total fat **17g**		
Saturated fat **5g**		
Sodium **350mg**		

250 g	wide egg noodles	8 oz
250 g	asparagus, trimmed, scraped, ends peeled	8 oz
3 tbsp	virgin olive oil	3 tbsp
1	onion, finely chopped	1
60 g	shiitake mushrooms, sliced, or 125 g (4 oz) button mushrooms	2 oz
2	garlic cloves, finely chopped	2
	freshly ground black pepper	
45 g	prosciutto, cut into strips 5 mm (¼ inch) wide and 2.5 cm (1 inch) long	1½ oz
1 tsp	fresh lemon juice	1 tsp
15	fresh basil leaves	15
60 g	Parmesan cheese, freshly grated	2 oz

Cut each asparagus stalk diagonally into three pieces, then halve each piece lengthwise. Set the pieces aside.

Heat 1 tablespoon of the olive oil in a large, heavy frying pan over medium-high heat. Sauté the onion until it becomes translucent — about 5 minutes. Stir in the mushrooms, garlic and some pepper, and cook the mixture until the mushrooms are tender — about 5 minutes more. If you are using button mushrooms, cook them an additional 4 to 5 minutes to evaporate some of their moisture. Add the asparagus pieces and cook them until they are tender — another 4 to 5 minutes. Stir in the prosciutto, lemon juice and basil leaves.

While the mushrooms are cooking, add the noodles to 3 litres (5 pints) of unsalted boiling water and cook them until they are *al dente* — approximately 9 minutes. Drain the noodles, and add them immediately to the frying pan. Add the Parmesan cheese and the remaining 2 tablespoons of olive oil, and toss thoroughly. Serve at once on warmed plates.

3 Rice and wheat noodles spill from drawers of Japanese chests in an Eastern setting that includes pungent ingredients associated with Asian pasta dishes.

The World of Asian Noodles

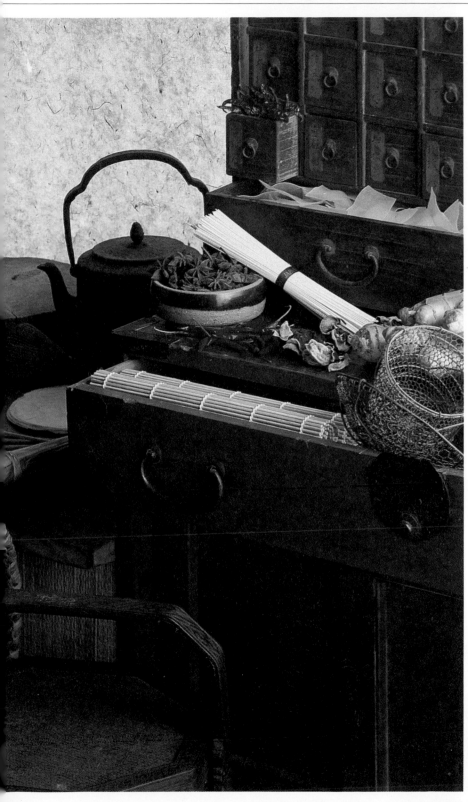

Only recently have many Western cooks made the happy discovery that there is a great deal more to pasta than the Italian kinds most people are familiar with — indeed, that there is a whole new world of pasta for them to explore. This is the world of Asian noodles and of the thin pasta wrappers that are used to cover egg rolls, spring rolls and other morsels. They take so many forms — and are of such major importance to cuisines as varied as the Japanese, Chinese, Thai and Indonesian — that it is a wonder they could have been overlooked for so long. Not only can they be bought in shops specializing in Oriental foods, but many are now available in supermarkets. Several, such as the wonton wrappers on page 113, can be made easily at home.

Fresh or dried, Asian noodles form the foundation of 20 of the recipes to be found in this section. The noodles are in no way mysterious. Produced from wheat flour, rice flour or vegetable starch, they come mostly in strings or strands, some curled into neat round or oval skeins. Whatever form they take, they are all temptingly appetizing in both texture and taste. Because rice noodles and vegetable-starch noodles are precooked as part of their manufacturing process, they need only be soaked in hot water in order to rehydrate them; occasionally they are boiled or simmered afterwards.

Fresh egg noodles and dried wheat pastas are cooked the same way as Western pastas — in lots of boiling water. They too should be tested regularly for doneness and served *al dente*. When fresh Chinese egg noodles are not available, substitute a dried Asian wheat noodle, or even a dried Western pasta such as vermicelli, spaghetti or linguine.

Techniques for finishing, serving and garnishing Asian noodles are described in this section as well. Among them are stratagems for re-creating the exciting flavours of Eastern dishes without incorporating the monosodium glutamate and excessive salt customarily associated with Asian food. Such tactics include reducing stocks and mushroom-soaking liquids, or building a flavour base from an infusion of such aromatics as ginger, garlic and lemon grass.

Less familiar ingredients are described in the glossary on pages 140-141 and can be bought in Oriental food shops. In many of the dishes, a number of different ingredients are used in sparing amounts to create a bouquet of flavours — a practice common to the new Western cooking and traditional Asian cuisines.

The recipes in this section thus tend to be longer than many appearing elsewhere in the book, and they are often more complex as well. But the reward will be dishes so complete in their satisfaction as to constitute meals in themselves.

A Panoply of Asian Pastas

WHEAT NOODLES

very thin wheat noodles
(somen)

flat wheat noodles

thin wheat noodles

wonton wrappers
wonton skins

gyoza wrappers

fresh egg noodles

nested wheat noodles

RICE NOODLES

MUNG BEAN NOODLES

rice-paper wrappers

cellophane noodles
transparent noodles
beanthread noodles

flat cellophane noodles
flat beanthread noodles

rice-noodle squares

All the Asian pastas called for by the recipes in this section are shown here. They have been divided into three basic categories and are identified generically; where appropriate, the Asian name most often associated with a pasta is also given. Since Asian pastas are likely to be sold under different names in a variety of languages, the cook would be well advised to learn what the three basic types look like and be guided by appearances when shopping.

rice vermicelli
rice sticks
(mifen)

flat rice noodles
thick rice sticks

Pancit Guisado

THIS RECIPE IS ADAPTED FROM A CLASSIC PHILIPPINE NOODLE DISH
RESEMBLING PAELLA. NAM PRIK IS A THAI CHILI PASTE, AVAILABLE
IN SEVERAL VARIETIES IN SMALL JARS IN ORIENTAL SHOPS.

Serves 6
Working (and total) time: about 1 hour

Calories **330**
Protein **31g**
Cholesterol **80mg**
Total fat **13g**
Saturated fat **3g**
Sodium **540mg**

350 g	fresh Chinese egg noodles, or 250 g (8 oz) dried vermicelli	12 oz
2 tsp	nam prik	2 tsp
2 tbsp	rice wine or dry sherry	2 tbsp
3 tbsp	low-sodium soy sauce or shoyu	3 tbsp
12	garlic cloves, 2 finely chopped and 10 thinly sliced	12
1 tsp	freshly grated lemon rind	1 tsp
175 g	pork fillet, trimmed of all fat, cut into 2.5 by 1 cm (1 by ½ inch) strips	6 oz
175 g	chicken breast, skinned, boned and cut into 2.5 by 1 cm (1 by ½ inch) strips	6 oz
250 g	prawns, peeled, tail of shell left intact	8 oz
2	slices streaky bacon, cut into thin strips	2
2	medium onions, thinly sliced	2
8	dried shiitake or Chinese black mushrooms, soaked in very hot water for 20 minutes, drained and squeezed dry, soaking liquid reserved	8

¼ litre	unsalted chicken stock, reduced to 4 tbsp	8 fl oz
1 tbsp	Chinese black vinegar or balsamic vinegar	1 tbsp
1 tbsp	finely chopped fresh oregano	1 tbsp
2 tbsp	finely chopped fresh coriander	2 tbsp
1 tbsp	fresh lemon juice	1 tbsp
3 tbsp	safflower oil	3 tbsp
1 tsp	finely chopped fresh ginger root	1 tsp
2	small courgettes, sliced diagonally into thin ovals	2
1	sweet red pepper, seeded, deribbed and sliced lengthwise into thin strips, each strip sliced in half diagonally at the centre	1
200 g	fresh bean sprouts, rinsed and drained	7 oz
4	spring onions, trimmed and chopped	4

In a large bowl, mix the nam prik with the wine, 1 tablespoon of the soy sauce, the finely chopped garlic and the lemon rind. Stir in the pork, chicken and prawns. Cover the bowl and allow the mixture to marinate at room temperature for at least 30 minutes.

In a wok or a heavy frying pan, cook the bacon over medium-low heat until it renders some of its fat — about 3 minutes. Add the thinly sliced garlic and sauté it with the bacon, watching that the mixture does not burn, until the garlic turns faintly golden — about 4 minutes. Add the onions and cook them, stirring occasionally, until golden and very limp — about 20 minutes.

While the onions are cooking, put 4 litres (7 pints) of water on to boil. Slice the mushrooms into thin strips. Reduce the reserved mushroom-soaking liquid over medium-high heat to about 4 tablespoons. Add the noodles to the boiling water. Start testing them after 3 minutes and cook them until they are *al dente*. Drain the noodles and keep them warm.

In a large saucepan, combine the mushrooms, reduced mushroom liquid, reduced stock, vinegar, oregano, coriander, the remaining 2 tablespoons of soy sauce and the lemon juice. Stir in the bacon-onion mixture and set the pan over very low heat to keep it warm.

Heat 1 tablespoon of the oil in a wok. Add the ginger and courgettes, and stir-fry them for 1 minute. Add the red pepper and bean sprouts, and stir-fry for 1 minute more. Toss the stir-fried vegetables with the bacon-onion mixture, then combine them with the noodles and transfer the mixture to a heated platter.

Wipe out the wok and pour in the remaining oil. When the oil is very hot, add the pork, chicken and prawns, and stir-fry for 90 seconds. Add the spring onions and stir-fry for 30 seconds more. Stir the meat and prawns into the noodles and serve immediately.

EDITOR'S NOTE: *This dish is equally tasty at room temperature. It may be prepared up to 2 hours beforehand and presented as part of a buffet. If you like, garnish it with lemon wedges, halved cherry tomatoes and oregano sprigs, and serve a fresh fruit salad with it.*

Eight-Treasure Noodles with Chinese Sausage

Serves 6
Working (and total) time: about 45 minutes

Calories **330**
Protein **20g**
Cholesterol **15mg**
Total fat **13g**
Saturated fat **4g**
Sodium **440mg**

250 g	dried flat wheat noodles or fettuccine	8 oz
1 litre	unsalted chicken stock	1¾ pints
1½ tbsp	safflower oil	1½ tbsp
1 tbsp	grated fresh ginger root	1 tbsp
1	small red onion, cut into 2 cm (¾ inch) squares	1
1	sweet red pepper, seeded, deribbed and cut into 2 cm (¾ inch) squares	1
3	lop cheong sausages, thinly sliced diagonally, simmered for 5 minutes in water to cover and drained, or 125 g (4 oz) barbecue pork (see editor's note, page 115), cut into 3 mm (⅛ inch) slices	3
175 g	mange-tout, trimmed and halved diagonally	6 oz
8	dried shiitake or Chinese black mushrooms, soaked in very hot water for 20 minutes, drained, stemmed and quartered	8
450 g	canned baby sweetcorn, drained, rinsed	15 oz
450 g	canned straw mushrooms, drained	15 oz
125 g	broccoli florets, blanched in boiling water for 1 minute, refreshed under cold water and drained	4 oz
150 g	cauliflower florets, blanched in boiling water for 1 minute, refreshed under cold water and drained	5 oz
2 tsp	cornflour, mixed with 2 tbsp water	2 tsp
1 tbsp	low-sodium soy sauce or shoyu	1 tbsp
1 tbsp	rice vinegar	1 tbsp
1 tsp	dark sesame oil	1 tsp

Reduce the stock to about ¼ litre (8 fl oz) and keep it hot.

Add the noodles to 4 litres (7 pints) of boiling water with 2 teaspoons of salt; start testing them after 3 minutes and cook them until they are *al dente*. Drain the noodles and rinse them with cold water.

In a hot wok, heat the oil over medium-high heat. When the oil is hot but not smoking, add the ginger and onion, and stir-fry them for 30 seconds. Put in the red pepper, sausage, mange-tout, shiitake or Chinese black mushrooms and baby sweetcorn, and continue stir-frying for 1 minute. Add the straw mushrooms, broccoli and cauliflower, and stir-fry until all ingredients are very hot — about 1 minute more.

Stir the cornflour mixture, soy sauce and vinegar into the hot stock. Pour this sauce into the wok and stir until it thickens, adding the sesame oil at the last minute. Put the noodles in the wok, toss them with the vegetables to heat them through, and then serve the dish immediately.

Imperial Garden Rolls

Serves 6 (18 rolls)
Working (and total) time: about 2 hours

Calories **275**
Protein **18g**
Cholesterol **55mg**
Total fat **1g**
Saturated fat **0g**
Sodium **555mg**

18	rice paper wrappers, about 15 cm (6 inches) in diameter	18
350 g	white crab meat, all bits of shell removed and discarded	12 oz
2 tbsp	fresh lime juice	2 tbsp
1	lime, grated rind only	1
½	hot green chili pepper (caution, page 33), seeded and very finely chopped (about 1 tsp), or ¾ tsp sambal oelek	½
1 tbsp	very finely chopped fresh mint	1 tbsp
1 tbsp	very finely chopped fresh coriander	1 tbsp
6	spring onions, trimmed and very finely chopped	6
60 g	cellophane noodles, covered with boiling water and soaked for 20 minutes, drained and cut into 5 cm (2 inch) lengths	2 oz
250 g	mange-tout, trimmed and thinly sliced lengthwise	8 oz
18	Chinese cabbage leaves, top 10 cm (4 inches) only	18
200 g	fresh bean sprouts, rinsed	7 oz
1	sweet red pepper, seeded, deribbed and julienned (about 36 strips)	1
3	red chili peppers (optional) — soaked in warm water for 20 minutes if dried — seeded and cut into 6 rounds (caution, page 33)	3
18	long spring onion greens for tying the packets	18
18	mint sprigs for garnish	18
18	coriander sprigs for garnish	18
	lime wedges for garnish (optional)	
Sweet chili dipping sauce		
1	garlic clove, chopped	1
2 tsp	sweet chili sauce	2 tsp
2 tbsp	fresh lime juice, including as much pulp as can be scraped out with a spoon	2 tbsp
2 tbsp	low-sodium soy sauce or shoyu	2 tbsp

For the dipping sauce, combine the garlic, sweet chili sauce, lime juice, soy sauce and 4 tablespoons of water in a small serving bowl.

To prepare the filling, combine the crab meat with the lime juice, lime rind, green chili pepper or sambal oelek, chopped mint, chopped coriander, chopped spring onions and the cellophane noodles. Refrigerate the filling for 30 minutes to allow the flavours to blend.

Meanwhile, blanch the mange-tout strips in 2 litres (3½ pints) of boiling water for 20 seconds and remove them with a slotted spoon. Use the same water to blanch the cabbage leaves and bean sprouts in separate batches for 20 seconds each. Refresh the blanched vegetables in cold water, drain them and keep them separate. Toss the bean sprouts with the crab-meat filling.

Arrange all the ingredients on a work surface. Set out two large plates, one of them filled about 5 mm (¼ inch) deep with warm water. ▶

To make a roll, immerse a rice paper wrapper in the warm water for 30 seconds and transfer it to the empty plate. Allow the paper to rest until it is uniformly soft. Arrange two red pepper strips and a few mange-tout strips on the upper half of the circle so that their tips overhang the edge. Mound about 4 tablespoons of the crab-meat mixture on top of the vegetables and carefully fold the bottom third of the sheet up over the filling. Fold in one side of the sheet, place a chili pepper round on the fold, then fold in the second side. Secure the roll by tying a spring onion green round it. Repeat the process with the remaining wrappers, vegetables and filling.

To serve as a main course, carefully place each roll on a cabbage leaf. Arrange three packets in the pattern of a fan on each of six plates and garnish them with the mint and coriander sprigs and the lime wedges, if desired. Dip the rolls in the sauce as you eat them.

EDITOR'S NOTE: *This recipe yields 18 individual servings for appetizers or a first course, or six main-course servings consisting of three rolls each. When serving the packets as a first course, accompany them with grilled fish. If the rolls are prepared in advance, keep them moist by misting them with water from a spray bottle.*

When buying rice paper wrappers, inspect them to ensure that only a few, if any, are cracked or flaked. Because the papers break easily when dry and may tear when moistened, handle them with care at all times. Store any unused papers in tightly sealed polythene bags at room temperature.

Chicken, Broccoli and Chilies on Egg Noodles

Put the chicken breasts in a pan and pour in enough water to cover them. Bring the water to the boil, then reduce the heat to low and poach the breasts until they are tender — about 10 minutes. Remove the chicken with a slotted spoon; discard the cooking liquid. As soon as the chicken is cool enough to handle, separate the meat from the bones. Discard the skin and bones and shred the meat by hand. Cover the chicken and set it aside in a warm place.

Add the noodles to 4 litres (7 pints) of boiling water with 2 teaspoons of salt. Start testing the noodles after 3 minutes and cook them until they are *al dente*. Drain the noodles, then rinse them with cold water and set them aside in a colander.

In a hot wok or a heavy frying pan, heat 1 table-spoon of the safflower oil over medium-high heat. Add the broccoli florets and stir-fry them until they turn bright green. Add 1 tablespoon of the rice wine along with the sugar, and stir-fry for 30 seconds more. Transfer the broccoli to a bowl, toss it with the sesame seeds and cover the bowl to keep the broccoli warm.

Heat the remaining safflower oil in the wok or frying pan until the oil is hot but not smoking. Add the chopped peppers and stir-fry them for 30 seconds. Pour in the soy sauce and the remaining rice wine, then add the chicken and the spring onions, and stir-fry the mixture for 1 minute more.

Pour boiling water over the noodles in the colander to reheat them. Divide the noodles between four serving bowls and ladle the simmering stock over them in equal amounts. Divide the broccoli and the chicken-spring onion mixture into four parts. In each bowl, arrange the chicken on one side and the broccoli on the other in a yin-yang pattern. Serve immediately.

Serves 4
Working (and total) time: about 35 minutes

Calories **305**
Protein **28g**
Cholesterol **30mg**
Total fat **14g**
Saturated fat **2g**
Sodium **455mg**

350 g	fresh Chinese egg noodles, or 250 g (8 oz) dried vermicelli or thin spaghetti	12 oz
½ litre	unsalted chicken stock	16 fl oz
3½ tbsp	rice wine or dry sherry	3½ tbsp
1 tsp	dark sesame oil	1 tsp
¼ tsp	salt	¼ tsp
	white pepper	
2	chicken breasts	2
3 tbsp	safflower oil	3 tbsp
150 g	broccoli florets	5 oz
¼ tsp	sugar	¼ tsp
½ tsp	sesame seeds	½ tsp
2	hot green chili peppers, seeded and very finely chopped (caution, page 33)	2
1 tbsp	low-sodium soy sauce or shoyu	1 tbsp
4	spring onions, trimmed and finely chopped	4

Bring the stock to the boil in a saucepan. Add 2 tablespoons of the wine, the sesame oil, the salt and some pepper, and return the liquid to the boil. Reduce the heat to low and let the stock simmer very slowly.

Nest of the Phoenix

THE CONCENTRIC RINGS OF VEGETABLES AND NOODLES
IN THIS SALAD SUGGEST THE RISING SUN, OFTEN SYMBOLIZED
BY THE PHOENIX.

Serves 8
Working (and total) time: about 1 hour and 15 minutes

Calories **355**
Protein **19g**
Cholesterol **75mg**
Total fat **5g**
Saturated fat **1g**
Sodium **295mg**

500 g	flat rice noodles	1 lb
600 g	cooked peeled prawns	1¼ lb
12.5 cl	fresh lime juice	4 fl oz
1 tsp	grated lime rind	1 tsp
3 tsp	sweet chili sauce	3 tsp
4 tbsp	chopped fresh mint	4 tbsp
1 tbsp	chopped fresh coriander	1 tbsp
250 g	mange-tout, stems and strings removed, blanched in boiling water for 1 minute, drained and julienned	8 oz
2 tsp	low-sodium soy sauce or shoyu	2 tsp
½ tsp	dark sesame oil	½ tsp
1 tbsp	chopped fresh basil	1 tbsp
1½ tbsp	safflower oil	1½ tbsp
2 tsp	finely chopped fresh ginger root	2 tsp
3	large carrots, peeled and julienned	3
6 tbsp	fresh lemon juice	6 tbsp
5	spring onions, sliced diagonally into very thin ovals	5
300 g	fresh bean sprouts, rinsed and drained	10 oz
3 tbsp	unsweetened coconut milk	3 tbsp
½ tsp	salt	½ tsp
1½ tsp	finely chopped fresh citrus leaf, centre vein removed, or 1½ tsp grated lime rind	1½ tsp
Garnish		
1	round lettuce	1
1	large sweet red pepper, seeded, deribbed and halved lengthwise, each half sliced crosswise into thin strips	1
	mint sprigs	
2	lemons (optional), each cut into 8 wedges	2

In a large bowl, combine the prawns, 2 tablespoons of the lime juice, the lime rind, 1 teaspoon of the sweet chili sauce, 1 tablespoon of the chopped mint and the ▶

tabespoon of chopped coriander. Set the bowl aside.

In another bowl, combine the mange-tout with the soy sauce, sesame oil and basil. Set that bowl aside too.

Pour enough boiling water over the noodles to cover them, and let them soak for 15 minutes. Drain the noodles and rinse them in cold water; drain them again thoroughly and set them aside.

While the noodles are soaking, pour ½ tablespoon of the safflower oil into a heated wok or a heavy frying pan over high heat. When the oil is hot, add the ginger and the carrots. Reduce the heat to medium and stir-fry the carrots for 1 minute. Add 2 tablespoons of water, cover the wok, and steam the contents for 2 minutes. Transfer the steamed carrots to a bowl and toss them with 2 tablespoons of the lemon juice. Set the bowl aside.

Wipe out the wok and heat the remaining table-spoon of safflower oil in it. Add the spring onions and stir-fry them for 30 seconds, then add the bean sprouts and stir-fry them for 1 minute more. Spread the spring onions and sprouts on a plate so they may cool.

Prepare the dressing for the noodles: in a large bowl, combine the coconut milk, salt and citrus leaf or rind with the remaining 6 tablespoons of lime juice, the remaining 2 teaspoons of sweet chili sauce, the remaining 3 tablespoons of mint and the remaining 4 tablespoons of lemon juice. Toss the dressing with the drained noodles and set them aside.

To assemble the nest of the phoenix, line a very large platter with the lettuce leaves. Fill the dish with the noodles, making a wide, shallow well in their centre. Tuck the red pepper strips between the lettuce leaves and the noodles all the way round the dish.

Arrange the carrots in a ring about 5 cm (2 inches) in from the edge of the noodles. Next make a smaller circle of the mange-tout just inside the carrot ring, then a ring of the onion and sprout mixture just inside the mange-tout. Mound the prawns in the centre and garnish the phoenix nest with the mint sprigs and the lemon wedges if you are using them. Serve immediately, at room temperature.

EDITOR'S NOTE: *If canned or frozen unsweetened coconut milk is unavailable, the coconut milk may be made at home: mix 3 tablespoons of unsweetened desiccated coconut in a blender with 3 tablespoons of very hot water and strain the mixture.*

Lobster Noodles with Treasures of the Sea

Serves 6
Working time: about 45 minutes
Total time: about 1 hour

Calories **285**
Protein **33g**
Cholesterol **70mg**
Total fat **9g**
Saturated fat **1g**
Sodium **515mg**

500 g	fresh Chinese egg noodles, or 350 g (12 oz) dried vermicelli	1 lb
1.25 kg	live lobster	2½ lb
150 g	trimmed monkfish fillets, cut into 12 equal cubes	5 oz
150 g	scallops (12 small scallops, or 6 large ones cut in half)	5 oz
6	courgettes (preferably 3 yellow and 3 green) scrubbed, each cut into 4 chunks, blanched in boiling water for 2 minutes and refreshed with cold water	6
Ginger-brandy marinade		
2 tsp	very finely chopped garlic	2 tsp
2 tsp	very finely chopped fresh ginger root	2 tsp
2 tsp	fermented black beans, rinsed and crushed	2 tsp
2 tbsp	brandy	2 tbsp
¼ tsp	salt	¼ tsp
1 tbsp	safflower oil	1 tbsp
Garlic-onion sauce		
1 tbsp	safflower oil	1 tbsp
1 tbsp	very finely chopped garlic	1 tbsp
1 tsp	very finely chopped fresh ginger root	1 tsp
5	spring onions, trimmed and finely chopped	5
2 tsp	fermented black beans, rinsed and crushed	2 tsp
¼ tsp	sugar	¼ tsp
1 tbsp	low-sodium soy sauce or shoyu	1 tbsp

Pour enough water into a 6 litre (10 pint) pan to fill it about 7.5 cm (3 inches) deep, and bring the water to the boil. Add the lobster, cover the pan, and cook for 5 minutes. Combine the marinade ingredients in a bowl and set aside.

Remove the lobster from the pan and set the lobster aside. Remove ¼ litre (8 fl oz) of the lobster-cooking liquid and reserve it. Add enough water to the liquid remaining in the pan to make about 4 litres (7 pints); set it aside for cooking the noodles.

When the lobster is cool enough to handle, twist off the tail section and the claws. Working over a bowl to catch the juices, pull apart the body and remove the tomalley, or liver, and the coral if there is any. Add them to the bowl and set aside. Cut the lobster tail in half lengthwise, then carefully remove the meat from the two halves (it will not be completely cooked); cut each half crosswise into six equal pieces. Add the tail meat, monkfish and scallops to the marinade, stir to coat the seafood, then let the mixture stand for 30 minutes. Remove the meat from the remaining pieces of lobster, dice it, and add it to the bowl containing the tomalley, coral and juice.

Preheat the grill and bring the reserved lobster water to the boil. Thread the seafood and courgettes on to 12 skewers in the following order: monkfish, courgette, lobster tail meat, courgette, scallop. Six of the skewers should hold green courgette chunks; the other six should hold yellow courgettes. Reserve any extra marinade.

Add the noodles to the boiling lobster water. Start testing the noodles after 3 minutes and cook them until they are *al dente*.

While the noodles are cooking, make the sauce. Pour the tablespoon of oil into a hot wok. Add the garlic, ginger and spring onions, and stir-fry them for 1 minute over medium-high heat. Add the black beans,

sugar and soy sauce along with the reserved lobster juice, tomalley, coral and diced lobster meat, the reserved lobster-cooking liquid and any remaining marinade. Stir-fry until the lobster is cooked — 1 to 2 minutes. Drain the noodles, add them to the wok, and toss them with the sauce.

Grill the skewers for about 4 minutes, turning them frequently to ensure even cooking.

To serve, arrange a portion of the noodles on each of six heated plates. Top each serving with two skewers and serve immediately.

EDITOR'S NOTE: *Fermented black beans are available from shops specializing in Asian foods.*

Pork-Filled Dumplings

Serves 8 as an appetizer (32 dumplings)
Working time: about 50 minutes
Total time: about 1 hour

Calories **160**
Protein **8g**
Cholesterol **40mg**
Total fat **3g**
Saturated fat **1g**
Sodium **80mg**

250 g	strong plain flour	8 oz
1	egg	1
¼ litre	unsalted chicken stock, mixed with ¼ litre (8 fl oz) of water	8 fl oz
Pork filling		
125 g	boneless pork loin, trimmed of all fat and finely chopped	4 oz
60 g	water chestnuts, chopped	2 oz
60 g	bamboo shoots, rinsed, drained and chopped	2 oz

1 tbsp	low-sodium soy sauce or shoyu	1 tbsp
2 tbsp	dry sherry	2 tbsp
1	spring onion, finely chopped	1
1 tsp	finely chopped fresh ginger root	1 tsp
2	dried shiitake or Chinese black mushrooms, soaked in very hot water for 20 minutes, drained, stemmed, squeezed dry and chopped	2
Chili sauce		
1 tsp	sweet chili sauce	1 tsp
1 tbsp	Chinese black vinegar or balsamic vinegar	1 tbsp
1 tbsp	soya bean paste	1 tbsp

To prepare the filling, combine the pork with the water chestnuts, bamboo shoots, soy sauce, sherry, spring ▶

Making and Shaping Wontons

1 *MIXING THE DOUGH. Sift the flour into a bowl and make a well in the centre. Lightly mix the egg with 4 tablespoons of cold water and pour this mixture into the flour. Mix together to form a fairly stiff dough.*

2 *KNEADING THE DOUGH. On a lightly floured surface, knead the dough by pushing it away from you with the heel of the hand, then folding the dough back on itself, turning it slightly as you do so. Knead for 5 to 10 minutes until very smooth.*

3 *ROLLING OUT THE DOUGH. Cut the dough into two equal pieces. Pressing firmly on the rolling pin, roll out one piece at a time to form a square approximately 36 cm (14 inches). The rolled out dough should be quite thin.*

 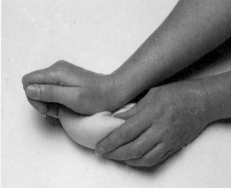 

4 *CUTTING THE WRAPPERS. Trim the pastry square to neaten the edges and cut it into 16 equal 9 cm (3½ inch) squares. Fill and shape the wontons (Steps 5 and 6), then repeat with the remaining piece of dough.*

5 *FILLING THE WONTONS. Put a heaped teaspoon of the filling into the centre of each square. Brush the edges with cold water to moisten. Fold each square diagonally in half to enclose the filling and form a triangle; press the edges to seal.*

6 *SHAPING THE WONTONS. Holding a wonton with the centre point away from you, gently bring the outer points round to plump up the filling and to meet in the centre. Moisten the outer points with cold water, then press together to seal.*

onion, ginger and dried mushrooms in a large bowl.

Make the wonton wrappers and fill them as demonstrated below.

Pour the stock into a pan large enough to hold the wontons in a single layer, and bring the stock to the boil. (If your pan is not big enough, cook the wontons in batches.) Gently lower the dumplings into the stock, then reduce the heat until the liquid is at a full simmer. Cover the pan and cook the wontons until their wrap-

pers are tender — about 7 minutes. With a slotted spoon, transfer the dumplings to heated plates.

Stir the chili sauce, vinegar and bean paste into the stock remaining in the pan. Pour some of this sauce over the dumplings and serve the rest separately.

EDITOR'S NOTE: *If you are using fresh water chestnuts, they should be peeled and trimmed of their dark spots before they are chopped and added to the filling.*

Barbecue-Pork Noodles with Emeralds and Rubies

Serves 4
Working (and total) time: about 25 minutes

Calories **375**
Protein **33g**
Cholesterol **45mg**
Total fat **16g**
Saturated fat **4g**
Sodium **555mg**

350 g	fresh Chinese egg noodles, or 250 g (8 oz) dried vermicelli	12 oz
1 tbsp	safflower oil	1 tbsp
250 g	Chinese barbecue pork, trimmed of all fat, and thinly sliced into pieces about 2.5 cm (1 inch) square	8 oz
1 tbsp	finely chopped fresh ginger root	1 tbsp
125 g	mange-tout, strings removed, sliced diagonally	4 oz
8	dried shiitake or Chinese black mushrooms, soaked in very hot water for 20 minutes, stemmed and sliced, the soaking liquid reduced to 4 tablespoons and reserved	8
150 g	fresh bean sprouts	5 oz
1	sweet red pepper, seeded, deribbed and sliced lengthwise	1
12.5 cl	unsalted chicken stock	4 fl oz
2 tbsp	low-sodium soy sauce or shoyu	2 tbsp

Add the noodles to 4 litres (7 pints) of boiling water with 2 teaspoons of salt. Start testing them after 3 minutes and cook them until they are *al dente*. Drain the noodles and keep them warm.

Heat the oil in a hot wok or a heavy frying pan over medium-high heat. Add the pork and ginger and stir-fry them for 2 minutes. Add the mange-tout, mushrooms, bean sprouts and red pepper slices and continue to stir-fry the mixture until the mange-tout turn bright green — about 2 minutes more.

Remove the pork and vegetables from the pan and set them aside. Add the drained noodles, the reserved mushroom-soaking liquid, the stock and soy sauce to the pan. Toss the noodles to combine them with the liquid. Return the pork and vegetables to the pan and mix gently. Divide the noodles between four large soup bowls and ladle over them any remaining liquid.

EDITOR'S NOTE: *Barbecue pork is a product available in Oriental food shops. If unavailable, it can be made at home by marinating a 250 g (8 oz) piece of boneless pork loin, quartered lengthwise, in a mixture of ½ tablespoon low-sodium soy sauce, ½ tablespoon dry sherry, ½ teaspoon dark sesame oil, ½ teaspoon finely chopped fresh ginger, ½ tablespoon honey and 1 finely chopped garlic clove. Refrigerate for 8 hours or overnight. Attach each strip to a paper clip unfolded into an S shape, reserving the marinade, and hook the clips on to an oven shelf; insert the shelf at its highest position in a preheated 180°C (350°F or Mark 4) oven. Set a pan of water below the strips to catch their dripping juices, and roast for 45 minutes. Baste with the remaining marinade, raise the heat to 220°C (425°F or Mark 7) and roast for 20 minutes more.*

Spicy Noodles with Pork and Peanuts

Serves 4
Working time: about 30 minutes
Total time: about 1 hour

Calories **320**
Protein **25g**
Cholesterol **20mg**
Total fat **15g**
Saturated fat **4g**
Sodium **525mg**

350 g	fresh Chinese egg noodles, or 250 g (8 oz) dried linguine	12 oz
1 tbsp	safflower oil	1 tbsp
2	spring onions, finely chopped	2
2 tsp	very finely chopped fresh ginger root	2 tsp
1	garlic clove, finely chopped	1
¼ to ½ tsp	crushed red pepper flakes or sambal oelek	¼ to ½ tsp
175 g	boneless pork, trimmed of all fat, finely chopped	6 oz
2 tbsp	dry sherry	2 tbsp
1 tsp	soya bean paste	1 tsp
1 tsp	hoisin sauce	1 tsp
1 tbsp	low-sodium soy sauce or shoyu	1 tbsp
4 tbsp	unsalted chicken stock	4 tbsp
4 tbsp	diced water chestnuts	4 tbsp
4 tbsp	dry-roasted unsalted peanuts, coarsely chopped	4 tbsp
¼ tsp	dark sesame oil	¼ tsp
1 tbsp	chopped fresh coriander	1 tbsp
250 g	cucumber, halved, seeded and julienned	8 oz
50 g	fresh bean sprouts	2 oz
4 tbsp	shredded or julienned radishes	4 tbsp
1	apple, peeled, sliced and tossed with 2 tsp lemon juice	1

Add the noodles to 3 litres (5 pints) of boiling water. Start testing them after 3 minutes and cook them until they are *al dente*. Drain the noodles, rinse them under cold water and set them aside.

Heat the safflower oil in a hot wok or a large, heavy frying pan over high heat. Add the spring onions, ginger, garlic and the crushed red pepper flakes or sambal oelek, and stir-fry for 30 seconds. Add the pork and continue stir-frying until the pork is no longer pink — about 3 minutes. Pour in the sherry along with the soya bean paste, hoisin sauce and soy sauce, then add the stock and the water chestnuts. Cook for 2 minutes before stirring in the peanuts and sesame oil. Add the noodles and toss them with the sauce until they are heated through — about 1 minute.

Transfer the noodles to a serving dish. Garnish with the coriander, cucumber, bean sprouts, radishes and apple. Alternatively, the garnishes may be served separately so that each diner may choose his own.

Warm Sichuan
Noodles with Spiced Beef

Serves 6
Working time: about 30 minutes
Total time: about 1 hour

Calories **280**
Protein **29g**
Cholesterol **30mg**
Total fat **12g**
Saturated fat **2g**
Sodium **340mg**

500 g	*fresh Chinese egg noodles, or 350 g (12 oz) dried vermicelli*	*1 lb*
350 g	*beef fillet or lean sirloin, trimmed of all fat*	*12 oz*
8	*dried shiitake or Chinese black mushrooms, soaked in very hot water for 20 minutes and drained*	*8*

4	spring onions, thinly sliced diagonally	4
1½ tbsp	safflower oil	1½ tbsp
Sesame-soy marinade		
4 tbsp	low-sodium soy sauce or shoyu	4 tbsp
2 tbsp	Chinese black vinegar or balsamic vinegar	2 tbsp
2 tbsp	rice vinegar	2 tbsp
1 to 2 tsp	chili paste with garlic	1 to 2 tsp
½ tsp	very finely chopped garlic	½ tsp
1½ tsp	very finely chopped fresh ginger root	1½ tsp
1 tsp	sugar	1 tsp
1 tsp	dark sesame oil	1 tsp
2 tbsp	safflower oil	2 tbsp
2 tbsp	toasted sesame seeds, crushed with a mortar and pestle	2 tbsp
5	spring onions, very finely chopped	5
30 g	fresh coriander, coarsely chopped	1 oz
Garnish		
1	small cucumber, scored lengthwise with a fork and thinly sliced	1
1 tbsp	toasted sesame seeds	1 tbsp
	coriander sprigs	

Combine the marinade ingredients in a bowl and set the marinade aside.

Cut the beef across the grain into julienne about 4 cm (1½ inches) long and 3 mm (⅛ inch) thick. Cut off and discard the mushroom stems, and slice the caps into strips about 3 mm (⅛ inch) wide. In a bowl, combine the beef, mushrooms and spring onions with one third of the marinade. Let the beef marinate for 30 minutes.

At the end of the marinating time, put 4 litres (7 pints) of water on to boil. Drain and discard any excess marinade from the beef mixture. Heat the 1½ table-spoons of safflower oil in a heavy frying pan or a wok; add the mushrooms, spring onions and beef strips, and sauté them for 1 minute. Set the beef mixture aside on a large plate, spreading it out so that it cools rapidly.

Add the noodles to the boiling water. Start testing them after 3 minutes and cook until al dente. Drain the noodles and transfer them to a large bowl. Add the remaining marinade and toss it with the noodles.

To serve, arrange the cucumber slices in an overlapping pattern around the edge of a large plate. Arrange the noodles in the centre of the plate, partly covering the cucumber. Make a shallow well in the centre of the noodles and spoon the beef mixture into the well. Sprinkle the sesame seeds over all and garnish with a few coriander sprigs. Serve at room temperature.

EDITOR'S NOTE: *A colourful salad of fresh fruit, tossed with unsweetened coconut milk and fresh lemon juice, and garnished with mint, makes a delightful accompaniment.*

Shining Noodle Salad with Beef and Tomato

Serves 6
Working time: about 30 minutes
Total time: about 1 hour

Calories **265**
Protein **16g**
Cholesterol **30mg**
Total fat **6g**
Saturated fat **2g**
Sodium **340mg**

250 g	flat cellophane noodles or rice noodles	8 oz
Two 175 g fillet steaks, trimmed of all fat		Two 6 oz
60 g	red onion, thinly sliced	2 oz
1	lime, grated rind only	1
4 tbsp	fresh lime juice	4 tbsp
2 tsp	finely chopped fresh coriander	2 tsp
2 tsp	very finely chopped fresh lemon grass, or 1½ tsp grated lemon rind	2 tsp
2 tsp	finely chopped fresh mint	2 tsp
½ tsp	finely chopped hot chili pepper (caution, page 33), or ½ tsp sambal oelek	½ tsp
½ tsp	finely chopped garlic	½ tsp
3 tbsp	low-sodium soy sauce or shoyu	3 tbsp
1 tbsp	safflower oil	1 tbsp
½ tsp	sugar	½ tsp
2	small round lettuces	2
3	ripe tomatoes, thinly sliced	3
	mint leaves for garnish	

Grill the steaks until they are rare and allow them to cool. Cut each steak in half lengthwise. Thinly slice each half into pieces about 3 mm (⅛ inch) thick, and toss the pieces with the onion slices. Set the mixture aside.

In a large bowl, combine the lime rind and juice, coriander, lemon grass or lemon rind, mint, chili pepper or sambal oelek, garlic, soy sauce, oil and sugar. Pour half of this marinade over the beef and onion slices, reserving the other half of the marinade for the noodles. Toss well, then cover the beef and let it marinate at room temperature for 30 minutes.

Pour enough boiling water over the noodles to cover them. Soak the noodles until they are al dente — 10 to 15 minutes, depending on their thickness. Drain the noodles, rinse them in cold water, and drain them ▶

once again. Wrap the noodles in a clean towel and squeeze out most of their moisture. Cut the noodles into 15 cm (6 inch) lengths and toss them with the reserved half of the marinade.

To serve, arrange some lettuce leaves on each of six plates. At one side of each plate, just inside the edge of the leaves, arrange several tomato slices in a crescent. Mound some noodles next to the tomatoes. Arrange the beef slices on top of the noodles, then distribute the onion strips round the beef in a flower pattern. Garnish the salads with the mint leaves and serve them at room temperature.

EDITOR'S NOTE: *To give the onion slices an intriguingly different shape, first halve an onion lengthwise, then cut one of the halves lengthwise into thin strips resembling crescents.*

Nonya Rice Noodles with Prawns

A BLEND OF CHINESE AND MALAYSIAN INGREDIENTS, NONYA DISHES ARE DISTINCTIVELY RICH AND SPICY. NONYA COOKING DEVELOPED IN THE 19TH CENTURY WITH THE INFLUX OF CHINESE TIN MINERS INTO THE MALAY PENINSULA.

Calories **350**
Protein **15g**
Cholesterol **60mg**
Total fat **8g**
Saturated fat **3g**
Sodium **360mg**

Serves 6
Working (and total) time: about 45 minutes

350 g	flat rice noodles	12 oz
350 g	fresh prawns, shelled	12 oz
2 tsp	very finely chopped fresh lemon grass, or 1 ½ tsp freshly grated lemon rind	2 tsp
1 tsp	very finely chopped fresh ginger root	1 tsp
½ tsp	very finely chopped garlic	½ tsp
½ tsp	salt	½ tsp
2 tbsp	safflower oil	2 tbsp
12.5 cl	unsweetened coconut milk	4 fl oz
35 cl	unsalted chicken stock, reduced to ¼ litre (8 fl oz)	12 fl oz
6 tbsp	fresh lemon juice	6 tbsp
2 tsp	low-sodium soy sauce or shoyu	2 tsp
2 tsp	sweet chili sauce	2 tsp
2 tsp	ground coriander	2 tsp
1	large onion, halved lengthwise and thinly sliced	1
1	sweet red pepper, seeded, deribbed and thinly sliced	1
1	lemon, cut into wedges (optional)	1
1	bunch watercress (optional)	1

Pour enough boiling water over the rice noodles to cover them, and let them soak for 15 minutes. In a large bowl, combine the prawns with the lemon grass, ginger, garlic and salt. (If you are using lemon rind in place of the lemon grass, set it aside for later use.)

Heat 1 tablespoon of the oil in a hot wok or a heavy frying pan over high heat. Add the prawn mixture and stir-fry it until the prawns are barely cooked — about 3 minutes. Transfer to a plate. Reserve any juices left in the wok, then wipe the wok clean.

In a saucepan, combine the coconut milk, stock, lemon juice, soy sauce and chili sauce. Bring the liquid just to the boil. Heat the remaining oil in the wok. Add the coriander and onion, and gently stir-fry them until the onion is limp — about 4 minutes. Add the red pepper and stir-fry the mixture for 1 minute more.

Drain the noodles and add them to the red pepper and onion in the wok. Pour in the coconut milk mixture and the reserved juices from the prawns. Cook over medium heat, stirring, until most of the liquid has evaporated. If you are using lemon rind in place of the lemon grass, add it now. Stir in the prawns and briefly heat them through. Serve immediately, garnished, if you like, with the lemon wedges and watercress.

EDITOR'S NOTE: *If canned or frozen unsweetened coconut milk is unavailable, the coconut milk may be made at home: mix 45 g (1 ½ oz) of unsweetened desiccated coconut in a blender with 12.5 cl (4 fl oz) of very hot water and strain the mixture.*

Burmese Curried Noodles with Scallops and Broccoli

Serves 6
Working (and total) time: about 35 minutes

Calories **280**
Protein **26g**
Cholesterol **25mg**
Total fat **9g**
Saturated fat **1g**
Sodium **440mg**

350 g	dried rice-noodle squares or other rice noodles	12 oz
3 tbsp	safflower oil	3 tbsp
1	large onion, chopped	1
3 tsp	finely chopped garlic	3 tsp
1 tbsp	finely chopped fresh ginger root	1 tbsp
1 tsp	ground turmeric	1 tsp
½ tsp	ground cumin	½ tsp
1 tbsp	ground coriander	1 tbsp
350 g	broccoli florets	12 oz
1½ tsp	grated orange rind	1½ tsp
4 tbsp	fresh orange juice	4 tbsp
2 tbsp	fresh lemon juice	2 tbsp
½ tsp	salt	½ tsp
350 g	scallops, each sliced in half horizontally	12 oz
4	spring onions, trimmed and finely chopped	4
250 g	fresh water chestnuts, peeled and sliced, or canned sliced water chestnuts, rinsed and drained	8 oz
45 g	thinly sliced shallots (optional), stir-fried in 4 tbsp safflower oil until browned and crisp, drained on paper towels	1½ oz

Heat 1 tablespoon of the oil in a hot wok or a heavy frying pan over medium heat. Add the onion, 1 teaspoon of the garlic, the ginger, turmeric, cumin and coriander. Cook, adding water as needed to prevent scorching, until the onion is soft and browned —about 15 minutes.

Heat 1 tablespoon of the oil in a frying pan over medium heat. Add 1 teaspoon of the garlic and cook it for 30 seconds, stirring. Add the broccoli, cover the pan, and cook the mixture for 3 minutes. Uncover the pan and continue cooking, stirring, until the broccoli is tender — about 1 minute more.

Meanwhile, discard any noodles that are stuck together. Cook the remaining noodles in 4 litres (7 pints) of boiling water with 2 teaspoons of salt. Start testing them after 5 minutes and cook them until they are *al dente*. Drain the noodles, add them to the onion mixture, and toss gently. Add the orange rind, orange juice, lemon juice and salt, and toss thoroughly.

Heat the remaining tablespoon of oil in a wok or frying pan. Add the scallops, the remaining teaspoon of garlic, the spring onions and the water chestnuts. Stir-fry the scallops and vegetables until they are barely done — 1 to 2 minutes.

Arrange the noodles on a serving platter. Distribute the broccoli around them, then spoon the scallops on to the noodles. Garnish the dish with the stir-fried shallots if you are using them, and serve immediately.

Prawn Pot Stickers

Serves 8 as an appetizer
Working (and total) time: about 1 hour and 30 minutes

Calories **210**
Protein **12g**
Cholesterol **25mg**
Total fat **9g**
Saturated fat **3g**
Sodium **275mg**

250 g	strong plain flour	8 oz
4 tbsp	safflower oil (for frying)	4 tbsp
Prawn filling		
350 g	cooked prawns, peeled and finely chopped	12 oz
4	dried shiitake or Chinese black mushrooms, soaked in very hot water for 20 minutes, drained, stemmed and chopped	4
250 g	fresh water chestnuts, peeled and finely chopped, or canned water chestnuts, rinsed, drained and finely chopped	8 oz
4	spring onions, trimmed and finely chopped	4
1 tbsp	finely chopped fresh ginger root	1 tbsp
2 tsp	finely chopped garlic	2 tsp
2 tsp	low-sodium soy sauce or shoyu	2 tsp
1 tsp	dry sherry	1 tsp
½ tsp	dark sesame oil	½ tsp
⅛ tsp	Asian chili sauce or Tabasco sauce	⅛ tsp
Hot dipping sauce		
2 tbsp	low-sodium soy sauce or shoyu	2 tbsp
2 tbsp	rice vinegar	2 tbsp
½ tsp	dark sesame oil	½ tsp
½ tsp	sugar	½ tsp
2 tsp	finely chopped fresh ginger root	2 tsp
1 tsp	finely chopped garlic	1 tsp
⅛ tsp	Asian chili sauce or Tabasco sauce	⅛ tsp
1 tsp	sliced spring onion	1 tsp

Make the dumpling dough as demonstrated in Steps 1 and 2 on the opposite page.

While the dough is resting, prepare the prawn filling and the dipping sauce. Put the prawns into a large bowl with the other filling ingredients and mix well. Cover the bowl and refrigerate the filling until you have prepared the dumpling wrappers.

In a separate bowl, stir together the dipping sauce ingredients and set aside.

Make the wrappers as explained in Steps 2 and 3, cutting only a few rounds at a time so that they do not dry out. Fill and shape them into pot stickers as demonstrated in Steps 4 to 6. (The dumplings can be made ahead of time and refrigerated on a lightly floured tray covered with plastic film.)

Cook the dumplings in two batches: pour 2 table-spoons of the safflower oil into a large, heavy-bottomed pan over high heat. Arrange half of the dumplings in the oil in a single layer without touching one another. Reduce the heat to medium and cook the dumplings until they turn golden-brown on the bottom. Add enough cold water to come two thirds of the way up the sides of the dumplings. Cover the pan part

Making and Pleating Pot Stickers

1 *MAKING THE DOUGH. Place half the flour in a bowl and add 5 cl (2 fl oz) of cold water to form a dry, crumbly dough. In another bowl, mix the remaining flour with 12 cl (4 fl oz) of boiling water to form a soft dough.*

2 *KNEADING THE DOUGH. Knead the hot-water dough on a lightly floured surface for 2 minutes, then gently work the two doughs together. Knead well for 5 minutes until very smooth and rest for 30 minutes. Divide the dough in two and roll each piece back and forth with your hands to form a thick roll about 4 cm (1½ inches) in diameter.*

3 *ROLLING OUT THE WRAPPERS. Cut three or four 1 cm (½ inch) thick rounds from one roll and flour their cut sides. Flatten each round with a small rolling pin, rotating it to produce a neat 9 cm (3½ inch) circle. Set the circles aside and cover with plastic film. Continue to make the circles a few at a time until the dough is used up.*

4 *ADDING THE FILLING. Put a heaped teaspoon of filling on each wrapper, slightly off centre. Brush round the edge with cold water. Fold the wrapper in half to enclose the filling and form a half-moon shape. Press the edges together to seal them.*

5 *PLEATING THE RIM. With your thumb and forefinger, gather two or three pleats on each side of the pot sticker, sealing the edge and allowing the filling to plump up. This creates a crescent shape.*

6 *CURLING THE CRESCENT. To give a sharper definition to the pot sticker, curl back its ends towards you and pinch them. Set it aside on a lightly floured surface and repeat with the remaining pot stickers.*

way and cook the dumplings until they have absorbed most of the liquid — 8 to 10 minutes. Remove the dumplings with a slotted spoon and set them aside on paper towels to drain. Transfer the dumplings to a heated serving platter. Cook the second batch the same way in the remaining 2 tablespoons of safflower oil. Serve the dumplings with the dipping sauce.

EDITOR'S NOTE: *Gyoza wrappers, available in Asian shops, may be substituted for the fresh dough in this recipe.*

Thai Chicken in Broth with Lemon Grass and Cellophane Noodles

Serves 4
Working time: about 30 minutes
Total time: about 1 hour

Calories **220**
Protein **18g**
Cholesterol **40mg**
Total fat **4g**
Saturated fat **1g**
Sodium **345mg**

60 g	cellophane noodles, tied together	2 oz
1.5 litres	unsalted chicken stock	2½ pints
250 g	skinned and boned chicken breasts	8 oz
30 g	cloud-ear mushrooms, soaked in very hot water for 20 minutes, then cut into thin strips (see note, page 125)	1 oz
3	stalks fresh lemon grass, bruised with the flat of a knife and knotted, or 1½ tsp grated lemon rind	3
2	citrus leaves, or 1 tbsp fresh lime juice	2
4	thin slices fresh ginger root	4
10	garlic cloves, peeled	10
2 tsp	fish sauce	2 tsp
2 tbsp	sweet chili sauce	2 tbsp
	fresh coriander for garnish	

Pour the stock into a heavy-bottomed fireproof casserole and bring it to the boil. Add the cellophane noodles, the chicken breasts, the cloud-ear strips, and the lemon grass and citrus leaves if using them. (If you are using lemon rind and lime juice, do not add them yet.) Thread the ginger slices and the garlic cloves on to skewers or wooden toothpicks, and add them to the stock with the fish sauce. Cover the casserole and remove it from the heat. Let the chicken stand undisturbed for 30 minutes.

Remove the chicken from the stock and set it aside to cool. Remove the lemon grass, ginger and garlic from the stock and discard them.

When the chicken is cool enough to handle, break it into shreds with your fingers. Remove the noodles from the stock, then untie them and cut them into 5 cm (2 inch) lengths. Reheat the stock; add the chicken, noodles and sweet chili sauce. If you are substituting lemon rind and lime juice, add them now. Ladle the mixture into individual bowls and garnish with the coriander leaves.

Beijing Wheat Noodles with Braised Lamb and Spring Onions

Serves 4
Working time: about 40 minutes
Total time: about 2 hours

Calories **395**
Protein **23g**
Cholesterol **35mg**
Total fat **21g**
Saturated fat **8g**
Sodium **405mg**

250 g	fresh Chinese egg noodles, or 175 g (6 oz) dried vermicelli	8 oz
2	bunches spring onions	2
2 tbsp	safflower oil	2 tbsp
250 g	boned lamb shoulder, trimmed of all fat	8 oz
4	large garlic cloves, sliced	4
¼ litre	unsalted lamb or beef stock	8 fl oz
12.5 cl	red wine	4 fl oz
1 tbsp	low-sodium soy sauce or shoyu	1 tbsp
1 tsp	chili paste with garlic	1 tsp
250 g	fresh water chestnuts, peeled and sliced, or canned sliced water chestnuts, drained and rinsed	8 oz
1	star anise	1

Trim and chop one bunch of the spring onions. Heat 1 tablespoon of the oil in a hot heavy frying pan over medium-high heat. Add the lamb and sear it until it is browned on all sides. Transfer the lamb to a heavy-bottomed 2 litre (3½ pint) saucepan or casserole and set it aside. Add the garlic and chopped spring onions to the frying pan. Stir-fry them over medium heat for 3 minutes, adding a little water if necessary to prevent sticking.

Pour the stock into the pan, scraping loose any bits that are stuck to the sides. Add this onion-stock mixture to the lamb in the saucepan. Stir the wine, soy sauce, chili paste, water chestnuts and star anise into the lamb mixture. Bring the liquid to the boil, then reduce the heat to low, and cover the pan. Simmer, turning the lamb once, until the meat is tender — about 1¼ hours.

When the lamb has finished cooking, put 4 litres (7 pints) of water on to boil with 2 teaspoons of salt.

Remove the lamb, water chestnuts and star anise from the braising liquid; discard the star anise. Reserve the liquid. When the meat is cool enough to handle, shred it by hand. Slice the remaining spring onions diagonally into thin ovals. Heat the remaining tablespoon of oil in a frying pan over high heat. Add the onion slices and stir-fry them for 1 minute. Stir in the lamb and water chestnuts; stir-fry for 1 minute more.

Add the noodles to the boiling water. Reheat the braising liquid. Start testing the noodles after 3 minutes and cook them until they are *al dente*. Drain the noodles, add them to the braising liquid, and toss them with the liquid; arrange them in a warmed dish and top with the lamb mixture. Serve immediately.

EDITOR'S NOTE: *Star anise, sold in dried florets resembling stars, tastes much like aniseed. Ground star anise is a component of Chinese five-spice powder.*

Duckling Dumplings and Ginger-Plum Sauce

CLOUD-EAR MUSHROOMS ARE ALSO CALLED TREE EARS, WOOD EARS AND BLACK FUNGUS. THEY COME IN SMALL CHIPS THAT OPEN INTO PETALS WHEN SOAKED IN HOT WATER. CUT AWAY THE TOUGH INNER PORTION BEFORE CHOPPING THE MUSHROOMS.

Serves 6 (36 dumplings)
Working time: about 1 hour
Total time: about 1 hour and 30 minutes

Calories **195**
Protein **19g**
Cholesterol **45mg**
Total fat **3g**
Saturated fat **1g**
Sodium **470mg**

36	wonton wrappers (recipe, page 113)	36
1 litre	unsalted chicken or duck stock	1¾ pints
	watercress sprigs for garnish	
Duckling-onion filling		
250 g	duck breast meat or turkey thigh meat, finely chopped	8 oz
2 tbsp	dry sherry	2 tbsp
1 tbsp	Chinese black vinegar or balsamic vinegar	1 tbsp
1	egg white	1
1	garlic clove, finely chopped	1
4 tbsp	chopped spring onions (about 2)	4 tbsp
1 tbsp	hoisin sauce	1 tbsp
6 tbsp	chopped water chestnuts	6 tbsp
2	dried shiitake or Chinese black mushrooms, soaked in very hot water for 20 minutes, drained, stemmed, squeezed dry and chopped	2
2 tbsp	cloud-ear mushrooms, soaked and very finely chopped	2 tbsp
	freshly ground black pepper	
Ginger-plum sauce		
1 kg	canned purple plums in heavy syrup, drained	2 lb
1 tbsp	cornflour, mixed with 2 tbsp water	1 tbsp
1 tsp	finely chopped fresh ginger root	1 tsp
1	garlic clove, finely chopped	1
¼ litre	unsalted chicken or duck stock	8 fl oz
1 tbsp	low-sodium soy sauce or shoyu	1 tbsp
1 tbsp	rice vinegar	1 tbsp
¼ tsp	salt	¼ tsp

Combine the filling ingredients in a large bowl.

To prepare the ginger-plum sauce, first remove the stones and skins from the plums, then mash their flesh with a fork (there should be about ¼ litre/8 fl oz of flesh). Put the flesh in a saucepan over medium heat and stir in the cornflour mixture. Add the remaining sauce ingredients and stir constantly until the sauce boils and thickens. Set the sauce aside.

Make the wonton wrappers as demonstrated on page 113, Steps 1 to 4. Add about 30 g (1 oz) of extra flour and a little water, if necessary, to allow for the larger number of wrappers.

Place about 1½ teaspoons of the filling mixture in the centre of a wonton wrapper. Using your fingers or a pastry brush, apply a thin film of water to two adjacent edges of the wrapper. Fold the wrapper into the shape of a wonton as demonstrated on page 113. Repeat the process with the remaining filling and wrappers, keeping the finished dumplings and unused wrappers covered with a damp towel to prevent their drying out.

Pour enough of the stock into a large, shallow pan to fill it about 2.5 cm (1 inch) deep. Bring the stock to a simmer, then gently add a batch of the dumplings to the liquid. The dumplings should form a single layer, with their sides barely touching, and the stock should cover them by about 1 cm (½ inch). When the stock returns to a simmer, partially cover the pan and cook the dumplings for 8 minutes.

With a slotted spoon, transfer the dumplings to a heated platter. Cover the dumplings with aluminium foil to keep them warm while you cook the remaining dumplings, adding more stock to the pan if necessary. Reheat the sauce.

Arrange half a dozen dumplings on each of six warmed plates. Garnish each with watercress sprigs. Serve immediately, passing the sauce separately.

EDITOR'S NOTE: *Both filling and sauce may be prepared up to 24 hours in advance and refrigerated until you are ready to use them. Broccoli spears stir-fried in ginger, soy sauce and sesame oil make a colourful accompaniment to the dumplings. Ready-made wonton wrappers, available from Asian shops, may be substituted for the fresh dough used in this recipe.*

Four-Season Dumplings with Sweet-and-Sour Sauce

Serves 6 as an appetizer
Working (and total) time: about 1 hour and 30 minutes

Calories **150**
Protein **12g**
Cholesterol **25mg**
Total fat **4g**
Saturated fat **1g**
Sodium **200mg**

175 g	gyoza wrappers, or wonton wrappers cut into circles	6 oz
175 g	lean pork, trimmed of all fat and finely chopped	6 oz
60 g	cooked prawns, peeled and finely chopped	2 oz
1 tbsp	dry sherry	1 tbsp
2 tsp	grated fresh ginger root	2 tsp
1	garlic clove, very finely chopped	1
3	spring onions, trimmed and very finely chopped	3
60 g	sweet potato or carrot, grated	2 oz
2 tsp	low-sodium soy sauce or shoyu	2 tsp
½ tsp	fresh lemon juice	½ tsp
2 tsp	very finely chopped fresh coriander	2 tsp
4 tbsp	diced water chestnuts	4 tbsp
2	dried shiitake or Chinese black mushrooms, soaked in very hot water for 20 minutes, stems removed, cut into 5 mm (¼ inch) squares	2
⅛	sweet red pepper, seeded, deribbed and cut into 5 mm (¼ inch) squares	⅛
2 tbsp	shelled peas	2 tbsp
	Sweet-and-sour sauce	
3 tbsp	frozen orange juice concentrate	3 tbsp
4 tbsp	unsalted chicken stock	4 tbsp
2 tbsp	fresh lemon juice	2 tbsp
2 tbsp	rice vinegar	2 tbsp
1 tbsp	oyster sauce	1 tbsp
1 tbsp	sugar	1 tbsp
1 tbsp	unsalted tomato paste	1 tbsp
2 tsp	cornflour	2 tsp

Combine the sauce ingredients in a small pan and stir them together until the cornflour is dissolved. Bring the sauce to the boil, stirring constantly until it thickens. Set the pan aside.

To make the filling, combine the pork, prawns, sherry, ginger, garlic, spring onions, sweet potato or carrot, soy sauce, lemon juice, coriander and 3 tablespoons of the water chestnuts in a large bowl. Place a scant teaspoon of the filling in the centre of a gyoza or wonton wrapper and form it into a dumpling *(technique, right)*. Garnish each of the four openings with one piece each of mushroom, red pepper, pea and the remaining water chestnuts.

Using a paper towel or a pastry brush, lightly oil the floor of a steamer. Arrange as many of the dumplings inside as will fit without touching. Cover the steamer, set it in a pot filled with 2.5 cm (1 inch) of boiling water, and steam the dumplings over high heat for 8 minutes.

Remove the dumplings and set them aside on a tray or serving platter; cover them with aluminium foil and put them in a low oven to keep them warm. Cook the remaining dumplings the same way, oiling the steamer floor before adding each new batch.

Meanwhile, re-warm the dipping sauce over low heat, stirring occasionally. Serve the dumplings hot; pass the dipping sauce separately.

EDITOR'S NOTE: *For home-made wrappers, use either the recipe on page 113 or that for pot stickers on page 120. To make a simpler variation of the dumpling, pull the outside edges of the filled wrapper in towards the centre, creating a cup; place a piece of each garnish inside the cup and steam the dumplings as directed.*

Fashioning Four-Season Dumplings

1 *SHAPING THE PIECE. Place the filling in the centre of a gyoza wrapper, or a wonton wrapper cut into a circle. Bring two edges of the circle together and pinch them at the top. Do the same with the other edges. Using a pastry brush or your finger, moisten the dough to make them stick, if necessary.*

2 *ADDING THE VEGETABLES. Flare out the openings. Drop a different vegetable filling into each. Repeat these steps to fill the remaining wrappers; then gently steam the dumplings.*

Ma Po Sichuan Noodles

Serves 4
Working (and total) time: about 25 minutes

Calories **305**
Protein **27g**
Cholesterol **30mg**
Total fat **13g**
Saturated fat **3g**
Sodium **470mg**

250 g	thin, dried wheat noodles or linguine	8 oz
250 g	lean pork, trimmed of all fat and diced	8 oz
2 tsp	fermented black beans, rinsed and drained	2 tsp
2 tbsp	dry sherry	2 tbsp
2 tsp	finely chopped fresh garlic	2 tsp
4	spring onions, thinly sliced	4
6	dried shiitake or Chinese black mushrooms, soaked in very hot water for 20 minutes, drained, stemmed and diced, soaking liquid reserved	6
2 tsp	hoisin sauce	2 tsp
2 tsp	low-sodium soy sauce or shoyu	2 tsp
1 to 2 tsp	chili paste with garlic	1 to 2 tsp
¼ litre	unsalted chicken stock, reduced to 12.5 cl (4 fl oz)	8 fl oz
1 tsp	cornflour	1 tsp
1 tbsp	safflower oil	1 tbsp
½ tsp	dark sesame oil	½ tsp

Combine the pork with the black beans, sherry, garlic and half of the spring onions. Let the pork marinate for 10 minutes. Meanwhile, in a large saucepan combine the mushrooms, their soaking liquid, the hoisin sauce, soy sauce, chili paste, and all but 1 tablespoon of the reduced chicken stock. Heat the mixture to a simmer.

Add the noodles to 4 litres (7 pints) of boiling water. Start testing after 3 minutes and cook until *al dente*.

Drain the noodles and combine them with the stock-and-mushroom mixture. Combine the cornflour with the reserved tablespoon of stock. Add this mixture to the noodles and simmer them for 3 minutes.

Heat the safflower oil in a hot wok or a deep, heavy frying pan over high heat; add the pork mixture and stir-fry it for about 1 minute. Turn off the heat, add the noodles and sesame oil to the pork mixture, and toss well. Arrange the noodles on a heated serving platter and garnish them with the remaining spring onions.

Japanese Summer Noodles with Prawns

Serves 6
Working (and total) time: about 45 minutes

Calories **200**
Protein **11g**
Cholesterol **40mg**
Total fat **1g**
Saturated fat **0g**
Sodium **225mg**

250 g	somen, or capelli d'angelo or vermicelli	8 oz
18	large prawns, peeled, the tails left on and the shells reserved	18
1	slice fresh ginger root, about 3 mm (⅛ inch) thick	1
1 tbsp	low-sodium soy sauce or shoyu	1 tbsp
3 tbsp	mirin	3 tbsp
6	dried shiitake or Chinese black mushrooms, rinsed	6
Garnish		
	watercress sprigs	
2	spring onions, thinly sliced diagonally, rinsed under cold water and drained (optional)	2
2 tbsp	grated fresh ginger root	2 tbsp
2 tbsp	wasabi, made by mixing enough water with 1½ tbsp wasabi powder to form a stiff paste	2 tbsp

Bring ½ litre (16 fl oz) of water to the boil in a saucepan. Add the prawns and the slice of ginger. Cover the pan, remove it from the heat and let it stand for 5 minutes. Strain the resulting stock into a second saucepan, reserving the prawns and discarding the ginger. Add the prawn shells to the stock and bring the liquid to the boil. Simmer the stock for 15 minutes, then strain it through muslin back into the first pan. Discard the shells. Reduce the stock to about 12.5 cl (4 fl oz) and let it cool. Combine the stock with the soy sauce and 1 tablespoon of the mirin, and divide this dipping sauce between six small bowls.

In a saucepan, pour 35 cl (12 fl oz) of boiling water over the mushrooms and let them soak for 10 minutes. Add the remaining 2 tablespoons of mirin and simmer until almost all of the liquid has evaporated — approximately 20 minutes. As soon as the mushrooms are cool enough to handle, remove their stems; cut the mushrooms in half, taking care not to squeeze out the liquid they have absorbed.

Add the somen to 1.5 litres (2½ pints) of boiling water; start testing the noodles after 2 minutes and cook them until they are *al dente*. Drain the somen, rinse them under cold water, and set aside in a bowl of cold water.

To serve, divide the noodles between six individual glass bowls. Put two or three ice cubes in each bowl, then pour in enough iced water (about 12.5 cl/4 fl oz) to float the noodles. Arrange three prawns and two mushroom halves on top of each portion of noodles. Garnish the bowls with the watercress and spring onions, if using. For each serving, place a bowl of noodles, a teaspoon of the grated ginger and a dab of wasabi on a large plate, with a bowl of the dipping sauce alongside.

EDITOR'S NOTE: *If you have access to a Japanese shop, substitute 12.5 cl (4 fl oz) of dashi — an infusion of dried kelp and bonito shavings — for the prawn stock in the dipping sauce.*

4 Topped with tomato sauce and redolent of fresh herbs, a slice of lasagne cooked by microwave reveals layers of spinach and cheese (recipe, opposite).

Pasta in the Microwave Oven

Microwaving might seem an inappropriate way to cook pasta. After all, does not pasta require lots of water to cook well? But the fact is that some pasta can be microwaved in relatively little water — or without any water at all when sauce or stock is substituted.

The trick is to provide just enough moisture for the pasta to absorb. The moisture renders it supple and produces the desired *al dente* quality of the boiled product. But the cook must still check for doneness to avoid the pasta turning soft and sticky. And remember that the food will go on cooking for several minutes after you have removed it from the oven.

The nine recipes that follow indicate precisely how much sauce, stock or water to include. (When cooking the pasta in water, be sure to use a deep enough dish so that the water will not boil over, and be careful not to burn yourself in the steam as you stir the contents, or on the hot dish as you remove it from the oven.) Some of the sauces can be prepared in advance in the microwave and added later.

Anyone who does not like having a big pan of water boiling away on the stove, especially on a hot and humid summer's day, will welcome the microwaving method. And in the two recipes that call for the sauce and pasta to cook together, there will be fewer dishes to clean up afterwards, and time will be saved as well, since the pasta need not be precooked.

Once cooks discover the ease of working with dried cannelloni tubes and lasagne (both of which tear all too readily when cooked conventionally), they may well become converted to the microwave technique. The cheese and sauce are spread on the lasagne before the pasta is cooked; the cannelloni are prestuffed and sauced. The proof, of course, is in the trying: you'll find recipes for lasagne layered with fresh spinach and for cannelloni filled with a three-cheese and parsley combination on the right and on page 138 respectively.

The recipes have been tested in both 625-watt and 700-watt ovens. Though power settings often vary among different manufacturers' ovens, the recipes use "high" to indicate 100 per cent power, "medium high" for 70 per cent and "medium" for 50 per cent. When using plastic film to cover a dish containing liquid, one corner should be left open to allow steam to escape, otherwise the build-up of steam may cause the film to explode.

Lasagne Layered with Spinach

Serves 8
Working time: about 20 minutes
Total time: about 1 hour and 15 minutes

Calories **300**
Protein **20g**
Cholesterol **40mg**
Total fat **13g**
Saturated fat **8g**
Sodium **410mg**

8	lasagne strips	8
30 g	unsalted butter	1 oz
1	medium onion, finely chopped	1
2	garlic cloves, finely chopped	2
125 g	mushrooms, wiped clean and thinly sliced	4 oz
800 g	canned tomatoes, drained and coarsely chopped, the juice reserved	28 oz
4 tbsp	tomato paste	4 tbsp
4 tbsp	red wine	4 tbsp
1 tbsp	chopped fresh oregano, or ½ tbsp dried oregano	1 tbsp
2 tbsp	chopped fresh basil leaves, or 1 tbsp dried basil	2 tbsp
2 tbsp	dark brown sugar	2 tbsp
½ tsp	salt	½ tsp
	freshly ground black pepper	
2 tbsp	freshly grated Parmesan cheese	2 tbsp
500 g	low-fat ricotta cheese	1 lb
1	egg white	1
500 g	fresh spinach, rinsed, stemmed, blanched in boiling water for 1 minute, squeezed dry and chopped	1 lb
250 g	low-fat mozzarella, thinly sliced	8 oz

To begin the sauce, put the butter in a 2 litre (3½ pint) glass bowl, cover it with a lid or plastic film, and microwave it on high until the butter is melted — about 1 minute. Add the onion, garlic and mushrooms, and toss them until they are coated with the butter. Cover the bowl again and microwave it on medium high (70 per cent power) for 2 minutes. Add the tomatoes, the reserved juice, the tomato paste, wine, oregano, basil, sugar, salt and some pepper, and stir well. Cover the bowl with a paper towel and microwave the contents on high for 12 minutes, stirring every 4 minutes. Stir in the Parmesan cheese and set the mixture aside.

In a smaller bowl, mix the ricotta with the egg white and some more pepper. Add the spinach and mix well.

Assemble the lasagne in a 25 cm (10 inch) square shallow baking dish. First spread 12.5 cl (4 fl oz) of the sauce evenly over the bottom of the dish. Lay four uncooked lasagne strips side by side in the sauce, then cover them with a thin layer of the spinach mixture and a layer of mozzarella slices. Repeat the layering pro- ▶

cess: spread half of the remaining sauce on top of the cheese, then cover it with the remaining lasagne, the rest of the spinach mixture and the last of the mozzarella. Top the dish with the remaining sauce and cover it with plastic film, leaving a corner open; microwave it on high for 6 minutes, then on medium high (70 per cent power) for 20 minutes more. Let the lasagne stand for 15 minutes before serving it.

Fettuccine alla Carbonara

Serves 4
Working (and total) time: about 20 minutes

Calories **440**
Protein **19g**
Cholesterol **90mg**
Total fat **18g**
Saturated fat **8g**
Sodium **470mg**

250 g	fettuccine	8 oz
100 g	lean rindless back bacon rashers	3½ oz
15 cl	semi-skimmed milk	¼ pint
10 cl	low-fat single cream	3½ fl oz
15 g	Parmesan cheese, freshly grated	½ oz
1	egg and 1 egg white	1
	freshly ground black pepper	
15 g	unsalted butter	½ oz
2	garlic cloves, crushed	2
	finely chopped parsley, to garnish	

Cover a large heatproof plate with a double thickness of absorbent kitchen paper. Arrange the bacon rashers in a single layer on the paper, then cover them with a double thickness of absorbent paper. Microwave on high for 2 to 2½ minutes until the bacon is cooked. Chop the bacon into small pieces and set aside.

Pour 2½ litres (4 pints) of boiling water into a large bowl, add 1½ teaspoons of salt and the fettuccine. Microwave on high for 10 to 12 minutes until the pasta is *al dente*, stirring every 3 minutes. Drain the fettuccine, cover and keep warm.

In a small bowl, lightly whisk together the cream, milk, Parmesan cheese, egg and egg white. Season with pepper, and set aside.

Put the butter into a large bowl and microwave on high for 30 seconds, until melted. Add the garlic and bacon, and microwave for a further 1 minute.

Add the egg and cream mixture to the garlic and bacon. Microwave for 2 to 2½ minutes, stirring every 30 seconds until the mixture is very hot, and slightly thickened. Add the pasta and mix well. Pour into a large warm serving bowl, sprinkle with parsley and serve immediately.

Pasta Shells with Clams and Sweetcorn

BEFORE STEAMING THE CLAMS, DISCARD ANY THAT
FAIL TO CLOSE WHEN THEY ARE TAPPED.

Serves 4
Working (and total) time: about 40 minutes

Calories **355**
Protein **17g**
Cholesterol **35mg**
Total fat **8g**
Saturated fat **4g**
Sodium **135mg**

250 g	medium pasta shells	8 oz
16	medium-sized clams, shells scrubbed	16
22 g	unsalted butter	¾ oz
2	spring onions, sliced diagonally into thin ovals	2
90 g	fresh sweetcorn kernels, or frozen sweetcorn kernels, thawed	3 oz
3 tbsp	plain flour	3 tbsp
15 cl	semi-skimmed milk	¼ pint
1 tbsp	paprika, preferably Hungarian	1 tbsp
⅛ tsp	cayenne pepper	⅛ tsp
2 tbsp	freshly grated Parmesan cheese	2 tbsp

Put 4 tablespoons of water into a 2 litre (3½ pint) bowl. Cover the bowl with a lid, or plastic film with one corner left open, and microwave it on high for 1 minute. Add the clams, cover the bowl again and microwave it on high until the clams have partially opened — about 2 minutes. Discard any clams that remain closed. Pour off and discard the water and leave the clams to cool.

Pour 1.25 litres (2 pints) of hot water into another 2 litre (3½ pint) bowl. Cover the bowl and microwave it on high until the water comes to the boil — about 7 minutes. Remove the cover, taking care to avoid the steam; add ½ teaspoon of salt and the pasta shells to the water. Replace the cover, leaving a small opening to vent the steam, and microwave the pasta on high for 2 minutes. Uncover the bowl, stir the pasta and replace the cover, again creating a vent. Return the bowl to the oven. Microwave it on medium (50 per cent power) until the shells are al dente — about 5 minutes more. Drain the pasta thoroughly and set it aside.

Put the butter in a 1 litre (2 pint) bowl and microwave it on high for 1 minute. Add the spring onions and sweetcorn, cover and microwave on high for 1 minute.

Shell the clams over their bowl to catch any juices. Allow the sediment from the clams to settle to the bottom of the bowl. Pour off 12.5 cl (4 fl oz) of the clam liquid and reserve it; discard the rest. Let the clams stand while you finish the sauce.

Whisk the flour into the onion-sweetcorn mixture, forming a paste. Gradually pour in the milk and the reserved clam liquid, stirring until the paste dissolves. Stir in the paprika and cayenne pepper. Cover the bowl and microwave it on high for 90 seconds. Uncover the bowl, stir the mixture, then replace the cover and microwave it on high for 90 seconds more.

Put the pasta shells and clams in a serving bowl. Pour the sauce over them and toss well. Cover the bowl and microwave it on high for 1 minute, then sprinkle the cheese over the pasta and serve at once.

Egg Noodles with Beef and Mushrooms in a Creamy Sauce

THIS RECIPE IS A LOW-CALORIE VARIATION OF
THE CLASSIC BEEF STROGANOFF.

Serves 4
Working (and total) time: about 20 minutes

Calories **435**
Protein **26g**
Cholesterol **100mg**
Total fat **14g**
Saturated fat **7g**
Sodium **445mg**

250 g	wide egg noodles	8 oz
2 tsp	safflower oil	2 tsp
15 g	unsalted butter	½ oz
250 g	mushrooms, wiped clean, stems trimmed, thinly sliced	8 oz
1	small onion, thinly sliced, the layers separated	1
250 g	beef fillet, cut into thin strips about 5 cm (2 inches) long and 1 cm (½ inch) wide	8 oz
1	garlic clove, finely chopped	1
1 tsp	dry mustard, mixed with 1 tsp water	1 tsp
1½ tbsp	paprika, preferably Hungarian	1½ tbsp
½ tsp	salt	½ tsp
	freshly ground black pepper	
4 tbsp	soured cream	4 tbsp
12.5 cl	plain low-fat yogurt	4 fl oz
4 tbsp	coarsely chopped chives	4 tbsp

Cook the noodles in the conventional manner: put them into 3 litres (5 pints) of boiling water on the stove top with 1½ teaspoons of salt. Start testing them after 7 minutes and cook them until they are *al dente*. Drain the noodles, toss them with the oil, and set them aside.

While the noodles are cooking, put the butter in a 2 litre (3½ pint) bowl and cover the bowl with a lid or plastic film. Microwave the butter on high for 30 seconds. Add the mushrooms and onion, and gently toss them until they are coated with the butter. Cover the bowl again and microwave the contents on medium high (70 per cent power) for 2 minutes. Add the beef strips, garlic, mustard, 1 tablespoon of the paprika, the ½ teaspoon of salt and a generous grinding of black pepper to the mushroom-onion mixture. Cover again and microwave on medium high (70 per cent power) for 5 minutes, stirring the mixture half way through the cooking time. Remove the bowl and drain off the liquid that has accumulated in the bottom.

Add the noodles, soured cream and yogurt to the bowl; stir well, cover the bowl and microwave it on high for 2 minutes, stirring after 1 minute. Transfer the mixture to a serving dish. Sprinkle the remaining paprika and the chives over the top and serve the dish hot.

Penne with Provençal Vegetables

Serves 4
Working (and total) time: about 40 minutes

Calories **335**
Protein **11g**
Cholesterol **5mg**
Total fat **7g**
Saturated fat **1g**
Sodium **185mg**

250 g	penne (or other short, tubular pasta)	8 oz
250 g	aubergine	8 oz
2	courgettes	2
2	sweet red peppers, seeded, deribbed and cut into 1 cm (½ inch) squares	2
3	garlic cloves, peeled and thinly sliced	3
2 tbsp	chopped fresh parsley	2 tbsp
¼ tsp	fresh oregano, or ⅛ tsp dried oregano	¼ tsp
¼ tsp	finely chopped fresh rosemary, or ⅛ tsp dried rosemary, crushed	¼ tsp
¼ tsp	fresh thyme, or ⅛ tsp dried thyme	¼ tsp
⅛ tsp	fennel seeds	⅛ tsp
¼ tsp	salt	¼ tsp
	freshly ground black pepper	
2 tbsp	virgin olive oil	2 tbsp
½ litre	unsalted chicken stock	16 fl oz
¼ litre	unsalted tomato juice	8 fl oz

Halve the aubergine and the courgettes lengthwise, then cut them lengthwise again into wedges about 1 cm (½ inch) wide. Slice the wedges into 2.5 cm (1 inch) long pieces. Put the pieces in a baking dish along with the red pepper, garlic, parsley, oregano, rosemary, thyme, fennel seeds, salt and some pepper. Cover the dish and microwave it on high for 2 minutes. Rotate the dish half a turn and microwave it on high until the vegetables are barely tender — about 2 minutes more. Stir in the oil and set aside while you cook the pasta.

In a deep bowl, combine the penne, stock and tomato juice. If necessary, add just enough water to immerse the pasta in liquid. Cover the bowl, leaving one corner open if using plastic film, and microwave it on high, rotating the bowl a quarter turn and stirring the pasta every 2 minutes, until it is *al dente* — about 15 minutes in all. With a slotted spoon, transfer the pasta to the baking dish with the vegetable mixture and stir to combine. Pour about half of the pasta-cooking liquid into the dish, then cover the dish and microwave it on high for 2 minutes more to heat it through. Serve at once.

Green Fettuccine
with Plaice

Serves 4
Working (and total) time: about 25 minutes

Calories **330**
Protein **19g**
Cholesterol **30mg**
Total fat **6g**
Saturated fat **1g**
Sodium **325mg**

250 g	green fettuccine	8 oz
4 tsp	virgin olive oil	4 tsp
2	garlic cloves, peeled and finely chopped	2
1 tbsp	chopped fresh oregano	1 tbsp
400 g	canned whole tomatoes, drained and coarsely chopped	14 oz
12.5 cl	clam juice or fish stock	4 fl oz
250 g	plaice or sole fillet, cut into bite-size pieces	8 oz
1/4 tsp	salt	1/4 tsp
	freshly ground black pepper	
2 tbsp	freshly grated Parmesan cheese	2 tbsp

Pour 1.25 litres (2 pints) of hot water into a 2 litre (3½ pint) glass bowl. Cover the bowl with a lid or plastic film left slightly open to allow the steam to escape, and microwave on high until the water comes to the boil — about 6 minutes. Stir in ½ teaspoon of salt and add the fettuccine; cover the bowl again and microwave it on high, stirring once after 3 minutes, until the pasta is *al dente* — about 6 minutes in all. Drain the fettuccine, then toss it with 2 teaspoons of the oil and set it aside.

In a shallow 1 litre (2 pint) dish, combine the remaining 2 tablespoons of oil with the garlic, oregano and tomatoes. Cover the bowl with a lid or plastic film and microwave the mixture on medium high (70 per cent power) until it is heated through — about 90 seconds. Uncover the dish and stir in the clam juice or fish stock and the plaice; cover the dish again, leaving a corner open, and microwave it on high until the fish is cooked through and can be easily flaked with a fork — 2 to 3 minutes.

Pour the fish mixture over the fettuccine, season with the ¼ teaspoon of salt and some pepper, and toss well. Cover the dish and microwave it on high until it is heated through — about 1 minute. Sprinkle the cheese over the top and serve immediately.

Spaghetti with Garlic, Oregano and Parsley

Serves 4
Working (and total) time: about 30 minutes

Calories **290**
Protein **8g**
Cholesterol **0mg**
Total fat **8g**
Saturated fat **1g**
Sodium **240mg**

250 g	spaghetti	8 oz
2	whole garlic bulbs, the cloves separated and peeled	2
¼ tsp	chopped fresh oregano, or ⅛ tsp dried oregano	¼ tsp
2 tbsp	chopped fresh parsley, preferably flat-leaf	2 tbsp
¼ tsp	salt	¼ tsp
⅛ tsp	cayenne pepper	⅛ tsp
2 tbsp	virgin olive oil	2 tbsp
1	lemon, cut into 8 wedges	1

In a baking dish, combine the garlic, oregano, parsley, salt, cayenne pepper and 12.5 cl (4 fl oz) of water. Cover with a lid or plastic film, leaving one corner open, and microwave the mixture on high for 6 minutes, turning the dish every 2 minutes. Remove the dish from the oven and let it stand for 2 minutes. Purée the mixture and set it aside.

Cook the spaghetti in the conventional manner: add it to 3 litres (5 pints) of boiling water with 1½ teaspoons of salt. Start testing after 10 minutes and cook until *al dente*. Drain and return to the pan. Pour in the oil and toss well. Add the garlic sauce and toss again. Transfer to a serving dish; garnish with the lemon wedges.

Put the butter in a 2 litre (3½ pint) bowl. Cover the bowl with a lid or plastic film and microwave it on high until the butter melts — about 30 seconds. Add the shallots, garlic, carrot and courgette; toss the vegetables to coat them with the butter, then microwave them on medium high (70 per cent power) for 4 minutes. Add the tomatoes and their juice, the tomato paste, oregano, basil, brown sugar, some pepper and the salt, and stir well. Cover the bowl loosely and microwave the contents on medium high (70 per cent power) for 12 minutes, stirring every 4 minutes. Set the sauce aside.

To make the filling, stir together the cottage cheese, mozzarella, egg whites, parsley and the Parmesan cheese. Using a small spoon or a piping bag with no nozzle, carefully fill the tubes with the mixture.

To assemble the dish, first reheat the sauce, if necessary, then spread half of it over the bottom of a shallow baking dish. Lay the filled cannelloni tubes in the sauce in a single layer and pour the remaining sauce over them. Cover the dish and microwave it on high for 10 minutes, then turn each tube over. Cover the dish again and microwave it on medium high for 17 minutes more. Uncover the dish and let the cannelloni stand for 12 to 15 minutes. Garnish with sprigs of fresh basil if desired.

Cannelloni with Cottage Cheese and Courgettes

TO ENSURE THAT THE PASTA WILL COOK COMPLETELY THROUGH, THE SAUCE MUST BE WARM WHEN YOU ASSEMBLE THE DISH.

Serves 6
Working time: about 35 minutes
Total time: about 1 hour and 30 minutes

Calories **380**
Protein **24g**
Cholesterol **30mg**
Total fat **11g**
Saturated fat **7g**
Sodium **590mg**

12	cannelloni tubes (about 250 g/8 oz)	12
30 g	unsalted butter	1 oz
3	large shallots, finely chopped (about 3 tbsp)	3
2	garlic cloves, finely chopped	2
1	medium carrot, peeled and coarsely grated	1
1	medium courgette, sliced into thin rounds	1
800 g	canned tomatoes, drained and coarsely chopped, the juice reserved	28 oz
4 tbsp	tomato paste	4 tbsp
1 tbsp	chopped fresh oregano, or ½ tbsp dried oregano	1 tbsp
2 tbsp	chopped fresh basil leaves, or 1 tbsp dried basil	2 tbsp
2 tbsp	dark brown sugar	2 tbsp
	freshly ground black pepper	
¼ tsp	salt	¼ tsp
350 g	low-fat cottage cheese	12 oz
125 g	low-fat mozzarella, coarsely grated	4 oz
3	egg whites	3
3 tbsp	chopped fresh parsley	3 tbsp
60 g	Parmesan cheese, freshly grated	2 oz
	fresh basil sprigs for garnish (optional)	

Tomatoes Stuffed with Farfallini

Serves 4
Working time: about 15 minutes
Total time: about 30 minutes

Calories **295**
Protein **15g**
Cholesterol **15mg**
Total fat **11g**
Saturated fat **6g**
Sodium **320mg**

90 g	farfallini (or other small, fancy pasta)	3 oz
4	large, ripe tomatoes (about 750 g/1 ½ lb)	4
30 g	unsalted butter	1 oz
1	small onion, chopped	1
½	sweet green pepper, seeded, deribbed and chopped	½
1	garlic clove, finely chopped	1
175 g	lean beef, minced	6 oz
½ tsp	salt	½ tsp
	freshly ground black pepper	
1 tbsp	curry powder	1 tbsp
1 tsp	paprika, preferably Hungarian	1 tsp
⅛ tsp	cayenne pepper	⅛ tsp
2 tsp	brown sugar	2 tsp

Put 1 litre (1¾ pints) of hot water and ½ teaspoon of salt in a 2 litre (3½ pint) bowl. Cover the bowl with a lid or plastic film, leaving one corner open, and microwave it on high until the water boils — about 5 minutes. Add the pasta and cover the bowl again. Microwave the pasta on high for 3 minutes, stirring it half way through the cooking time. Test the pasta; if it is not yet *al dente*, microwave it for 1 minute more and test again. Drain the pasta and set it aside.

Remove and discard the tops of the tomatoes. With a teaspoon, scoop out the flesh of each tomato and set the cases aside. Chop the flesh, add it to the pasta, and toss well together.

In a larger, covered bowl, microwave the butter on high for 30 seconds. Add the onion, green pepper and garlic, and toss them until they are coated with the butter. Cover the bowl again and microwave it on high for 90 seconds.

Crumble the beef on to a glass plate and season it with ¼ teaspoon of the salt and some black pepper. Cover the plate with a paper towel and microwave the beef on high for a total of 90 seconds, stirring after 45 seconds.

Spoon the cooked beef into the bowl with the onion mixture and discard the liquid remaining on the plate. Add the pasta-tomato mixture and the curry powder, paprika, cayenne pepper and sugar, and stir thoroughly. Season the inside of each tomato with the remaining ¼ teaspoon of salt and some black pepper. Stuff each tomato loosely with the beef-and-pasta mixture.

Arrange the stuffed tomatoes around the edge of a plate. Cover them with plastic film and microwave them on medium high (70 per cent power) for 7 minutes, turning each tomato a half turn midway through the cooking time. Remove the tomatoes from the oven and let them stand, still covered, for 2 minutes before serving.

Glossary

Asian egg noodles: long, toothsome wheat pasta available fresh, frozen or dried in Asian shops. Fresh noodles may be refrigerated for up to five days; when frozen, they should be cooked without being thawed.

Balsamic vinegar: a mild, intensely fragrant wine-based vinegar.

Bean sprouts: the sprouts of green mung beans. Use only fresh bean sprouts; canned bean sprouts are often mushy.

Beanthread noodles: see Cellophane noodles.

Black vinegar, Chinese (also called Chenkong vinegar, Chinkiang vinegar): a dark vinegar made from fermented rice.

Blanch: to partially cook food by briefly immersing it in boiling water.

Buckwheat: the seed of the flowering buckwheat plant. Buckwheat groats (also called kasha) are hulled, steamed, dried and sometimes toasted to intensify flavour. Buckwheat flour is unrelated to wheat flour and lacks the proteins required to form gluten.

Bulb fennel: see Fennel.

Burghul (also called bulgur): a type of cracked wheat, where the kernels are steamed and dried before being crushed.

Calorie (or kilocalorie): a precise measure of the energy food supplies when it is broken down for use in the body.

Cardamom: the bittersweet, aromatic dried seeds or whole pods of a plant in the ginger family. Often used in curries.

Cellophane noodles (also called beanthread noodles, glass noodles, harusame, mung-bean noodles, saifun and transparent noodles): an Asian pasta made from various vegetable starches, most often that of mung beans. Available in forms ranging from small skeins to 500 g (1 lb) packages of loose noodles, cellophane noodles should be soaked in hot water until they are soft.

Chiffonade: a leafy vegetable sliced into very thin shreds.

Chili paste: a paste made from chili peppers, salt and other ingredients; among its variations are chili paste with garlic and chili paste with black beans.

Chili pepper: a variety of hot red, yellow or green pepper. Finger-like Asian chili peppers are much hotter than Western chilies. Tiny Thai chilies are especially fiery. Fresh or dried, chili peppers contain volatile oils than can irritate the skin and eyes; they must be handled with extreme care (caution, page 33). See also Sambal oelek.

Chili sauce, Asian: see Chili paste; Sambal oelek; Sweet chili sauce; Tabasco sauce.

Chinese black mushrooms: dark dried mushrooms with a deep, smoky flavour. The larger mushrooms with cracked surfaces are considered best. Like any dried mushrooms, they must be soaked and stemmed. See also Mushrooms, dried Asian.

Chinese black vinegar: see Black vinegar, Chinese.

Chinese sausage: a small, thin, hard sausage available in Asian shops. It should be steamed or simmered before use. To store Chinese sausage, refrigerate it for up to one month or freeze it. Chinese pork sausage — lop cheong — tastes sweetly savoury.

Cholesterol: a waxy, fatlike substance that is manufactured in the human body and is also found in foods of animal origin. Although a certain amount of cholesterol is necessary for the body to function properly, an excess can accumulate in the arteries, contributing to heart disease. See also Monounsaturated fat; Polyunsaturated fat; Saturated fat.

Cilantro: see Coriander

Citrus leaves (lime leaves): the leaves of the kaffir lime tree, used in South-East Asian cuisine for their distinctive flavour. Citrus leaves are available fresh, frozen and dried in Asian shops; if you cannot find any, substitute fresh lime or lemon leaves, lime juice or pared lime rind.

Cloud-ear mushrooms (also called tree ears, tree fungus, mo-er and wood ears): silver-edged, flavourless lichen used primarily for their crunchy texture and dark colour. Cloud ears expand much more than other mushrooms when soaked. See also Mushrooms, dried Asian.

Coconut milk, unsweetened: a liquid extracted from fresh or dried coconut meat. Unsweetened coconut milk can be purchased either canned or frozen. Because of its high saturated-fat content, coconut milk should be used sparingly.

Coriander (also called cilantro): the pungent peppery leaves of the coriander plant or its earthy tasting dried seeds. It is a common seasoning in Middle-Eastern, Oriental and Latin-American cookery.

Cumin: the seeds of a plant related to caraway. The raw seeds add a pleasantly bitter flavour to curry and chili powders; when toasted, they have a nutty taste.

Dark sesame oil: a dark seasoning oil made from toasted sesame seeds, high in polyunsaturated fats, with a nutty, smoky aroma. Because the oil has a relatively low smoking point, it is rarely heated.

Fennel: a herb (also called wild fennel) whose feathery leaves and dried seeds have a mild anise flavour and are much used for flavouring. Its vegetable relative, the bulb — or Florence — fennel (also called finocchio) can be cooked, or eaten raw in salads.

Fermented black beans: soya beans that have been fermented, dried and salted. The beans should be rinsed and crushed before use.

Fish sauce (also called nuoc mam and nam pla): a thin, brown, salty liquid made from fermented fish. It is used in South-East Asian cooking to bring out the flavours of a dish. If fish sauce is not available, substitute a mixture of one part anchovy paste to four parts water.

Ginger: the spicy, buff-coloured, rootlike stem of the ginger plant, used as a seasoning either fresh or dried and powdered. The dried form should never be substituted for the fresh.

Gluten: the protein in wheat and other cereals which becomes elastic when wet and holds dough together.

Gyoza wrappers: circular wonton wrappers.

Hoisin sauce: a thick, dark, reddish-brown sauce generally made from soya beans, flour, garlic, sugar and spices. It is best known as the accompaniment to Peking duck.

Julienne: the French term for vegetables or other food cut into strips.

Kasha: see Buckwheat.

Lemon grass (citronella): a long, woody, lemon-flavoured stalk that is shaped like a spring onion. Lemon grass is available in Asian shops. To store it, refrigerate in plastic film for up to two weeks; lemon grass may also be frozen for storage.

Lop cheong: see Chinese sausage.

Mange-tout: flat green pea pods eaten whole, with only stems and strings removed.

Mifen: see Rice noodles.

Mirin: a sweetened Japanese cooking wine that is made from rice. If mirin is unavailable, substitute a mixture of equal parts sugar and sake, dry sherry or white wine.

Monounsaturated fats: one of the three types of fats found in foods. Monounsaturated fats are believed not to raise the level of cholesterol in the blood.

Mung-bean noodles: see Cellophane noodles.

Mushrooms, dried Asian: before use, dried Asian mushrooms must be soaked in very hot or boiling water for at least 20 minutes, then trimmed of their woody stems. To use the mushroom-soaking liquid as a flavouring agent, pour off and reserve the clear liquid; discard any sand that settles to the bottom. Soaked mushrooms can be stored in plastic film in the refrigerator. See also Chinese black mushrooms; Cloud-ear mushrooms; Shiitake mushrooms; Straw mushrooms.

Non-reactive pan: a cooking vessel whose surface does not chemically react with food. Materials used include stainless steel, enamel, glass and some alloys. Untreated cast iron and aluminium may react with acids, producing discoloration or a peculiar taste.

Olive oil: any of various grades of cooking oil extracted from olives. Extra virgin olive oil has a full, fruity flavour and very low acidity. Virgin olive oil is lighter in flavour and slightly higher in acidity. Pure olive oil, a processed blend of olive oils, has the lightest taste and the highest acidity. To prevent rancidity, the oil should be stored in a cool, dark place.

Oyster sauce: a savoury sauce made from oyster extract and seasonings, used to impart a subtle richness in Chinese dishes.

Pine-nuts: seeds from the cone of the stone pine, a tree native to the Mediterranean. Pine-nuts are used in pesto and other sauces; their buttery flavour can be heightened by light toasting.

Polyunsaturated fats: one of the three types of fat found in foods. They exist in abundance in such vegetable oils as safflower, sunflower, corn and soya bean. Polyunsaturated fats lower the level of cholesterol in the blood.

Puréed tomatoes: purée made from skinned fresh or canned tomatoes. Available commercially, but should not be confused with the thicker concentrated tomato paste sometimes labelled tomato purée.

Radicchio: red chicory.

Recommended Daily Amount (RDA): the average daily amount of an essential nutrient recommended for healthy people by the U.K. Department of Health and Social Security.

Reduce: to boil down a liquid in order to concentrate its flavour and thicken its consistency.

Refresh: to rinse a vegetable under cold water in order to arrest its cooking and set its colour.

Rice noodles (also called mifen): an Asian pasta made from rice starch. Rice noodles are available as flat noodles, as thin vermicelli (also called rice sticks), as squares, or as wrappers called rice papers. All but rice papers must be soaked in very hot water or boiled; rice papers need only be dipped in warm water to soften them.

Rice vinegar: a mild, fragrant vinegar that is less assertive than cider vinegar and not as harsh as distilled white vinegar. It is available in dark, light, seasoned and sweetened varieties. Japanese rice vinegar is generally milder than the Chinese variety.

Rice wine: Chinese rice wine (shao-hsing) is brewed from rice and wine. Japanese rice wine (sake) has a different flavour, but it may be used as a substitute. If rice wine is unavailable, use dry sherry in its place. See also Mirin.

Rocket (also called arugula): a peppery-flavoured salad plant with long, leafy stems, popular in Italy.

Safflower oil: a vegetable oil that contains a high proportion of polyunsaturated fats.

Saffron: the dried, yellowish-red stigmas (or threads) of the saffron crocus, which yield a powerful yellow colour as well as a pungent flavour. Powdered saffron may be substituted for the threads but has less flavour.

Sambal oelek: an Indonesian sauce made from chili peppers. It is available in Asian shops. Sambal oelek makes an excellent substitute for fresh or dried chili peppers.

Saturated fats: one of the three types of fat found in foods. They exist in abundance in animal products and coconut and palm oils; they raise the level of cholesterol in the blood. Because high blood-cholesterol levels may cause heart disease, saturated fat consumption should be restricted to less than 15 per cent of the calories provided by the daily diet.

Sauté: to cook a food quickly in a small amount of oil over high heat.

Semolina: the ground endosperm of kernels of durum wheat. Fine semolina makes a pasta of excellent resilience and body.

Sesame oil: see Dark sesame oil.

Shiitake mushrooms: a variety of mushroom originally cultivated only in Japan, that is sold fresh or dried. Dried shiitake mushrooms should be soaked and stemmed before they are used. See also Mushrooms, dried Asian.

Sodium: a nutrient essential to maintaining the proper balance of fluids in the body. In most diets, a major source of the element is table salt, made up of 40 per cent sodium. Excess sodium may contribute to high blood pressure, which increases the risk of heart disease. One teaspoon (5.5 g) of salt, with 2,132 milligrams of sodium, contains just over the maximum daily amount recommended by the World Health Organization.

Soya bean paste (or bean sauce): a thick brown paste made from soya beans, spices and salt.

Soy sauce: a savoury, salty brown liquid made from fermented soya beans and available in both light and dark versions. One tablespoon of ordinary soy sauce contains 1,030 milligrams of sodium; lower-sodium variations, such as naturally-fermented shoyu, may contain half that amount.

Somen: a very fine, white Japanese wheat noodle.

Star anise: a woody, star-shaped spice, similar in flavour to anise seed and used most often in braised dishes. Ground star anise is a component of Chinese five-spice powder.

Stir-fry: to cook thin slices of vegetables, fish or meat over high heat in a small amount of oil, stirring constantly to ensure even cooking in a short time. The traditional cooking vessel is a Chinese wok; a heavy-bottomed frying pan may also be used.

Stock: a savoury liquid made by simmering aromatic vegetables, herbs and spices — and usually uncooked meat, bones and trimmings — in water. Stock forms a flavour-rich base for sauces.

Straw mushrooms: cultivated type of mushroom with pointed caps and a silky texture. Straw mushrooms are usually available in cans or jars; the dried variety must be soaked in very hot water for at least 20 minutes before use. See also Mushrooms, dried Asian.

Sugar snap peas: a variation of garden peas, introduced comparatively recently. Once stem and string are removed the entire pod may be eaten, even when fully mature.

Sun-dried tomatoes: tomatoes that have been naturally dried in the sun, then preserved in oil and seasoning, usually including herbs. Sold in jars or cans and used to garnish pasta, pizza or salads.

Sweet chili sauce: any of a group of Asian sauces containing chilies, vinegar, garlic, sugar and salt. The sauce may be used as a condiment to accompany meats, poultry or fish, or it may be included as an ingredient in a dish. Thai varieties, which include seeds and small pieces of chili, are far milder than the ketchup-like sweet chili sauces produced in Malaysia and Singapore. When sweet chili sauce is unavailable, make it at home by mixing 1 tablespoon each of golden syrup and rice vinegar with 1 to 2 teaspoons of crushed red pepper flakes.

Sweet potato: either one of two types of nutritious tuber, one with yellowish mealy flesh, the other with a moist, sweet, orange flesh. The latter is often sold as yam but should not be confused with the true yam, see below.

Tabasco sauce: a hot, unsweetened chili sauce. A similar Asian version is the Thai sriracha sauce.

Tarragon: a strong herb with a sweet anise taste. Because heat intensifies tarragon's flavour, cooked dishes require smaller amounts.

Thyme: a versatile herb with a zesty, slightly 'fruity' flavour and a strong aroma.

Tomato paste: a concentrated tomato purée, available in cans and tubes, used in sauces and soups. See also Puréed tomatoes.

Total fat: an individual's daily intake of polyunsaturated, monounsaturated and saturated fats. Nutritionists recommend that fats provide no more than 35 per cent of the energy in the diet. The term as used in this book refers to the combined fats in a given dish or food.

Transparent noodles: see Cellophane noodles.

Turmeric: a yellow spice from a plant related to ginger, used as a colouring agent and occasionally as a substitute for saffron. Turmeric has a musty odour and a slightly bitter flavour.

Virgin olive oil: see Olive oil.

Wasabi: a Japanese horseradish root, usually sold in powdered form. It is mixed with water to form a fiery green paste, served with noodles or sushi.

Water chestnut: the walnut-size tuber of an aquatic Asian plant, with rough brown skin and white, sweet, crisp flesh. Fresh water chestnuts may be refrigerated for up to two weeks; they must be peeled before use. To store canned water chestnuts, first blanch or rinse them, then refrigerate for as long as three weeks in fresh water changed daily. A crisp, mild vegetable such as Jerusalem artichoke makes an acceptable substitute.

White pepper: a powder ground from the same dried berry as that used to make black pepper, but with the berry's outer shell removed before grinding, resulting in a milder flavour.

Wonton wrapper: a thin dough wrapper, about 9 cm (3½ inches) square, made of wheat flour and egg; it is used to encase spicy fillings of meat, fish or vegetables.

Yam: a number of varieties of hairy tuber, rich in vitamin A and similar in taste, when cooked, to the potato. Sometimes known as the Indian potato, it should not be confused with the sweet potato, which is sometimes also sold as yam. The yam is less sweet and less widely available than the sweet potato.

Index

Picture Credits

All photographs in this volume were taken by staff photographer Renée Comet unless otherwise indicated below:

Cover: James Murphy. 2: top and centre, Carolyn Wall Rothery. 4: lower left, Michael Latil. 5: upper right, Michael Latil. 9: Rina Ganassa. 12-13: Taran Z. 18: top, Steven Biver; bottom, Taran Z. 20: right,

Taran Z. 21, 22: Steven Biver. 23: top, Taran Z; bottom, Steven Biver. 25: Steven Biver. 26: left, Michael Latil; right, Taran Z. 27: Steven Biver. 30: Michael Latil. 32: Steven Biver. 36: Michael Latil. 38: Steven Biver. 39: top, Taran Z; bottom, Steven Biver. 44-45: Taran Z. 51: top, Michael Latil. 60: bottom, Michael Latil. 61: Karan Knauer. 67: Michael Latil. 72: Aldo Tutino. 84: top, Michael Latil. 90: John Elliott.

92: John Elliott. 94: John Elliott. 96: John Elliott. 99: Taran Z. 102-103: Taran Z. 105: Michael Latil. 108: Michael Latil. 111-112: Michael Latil. 113: John Elliott. 115: Michael Latil. 119, 120: Michael Latil. 121: John Elliott. 122, 123: Michael Latil. 126: Michael Latil. 127: Taran Z. 129,130: Michael Latil. 132: John Elliott. 133-136: Michael Latil. 138, 139: Michael Latil.

Acknowledgements

The editors are particularly indebted to Mary Jane Blandford, Alexandria, Va., U.S.A.; Nora Carey, Paris; Chong Su Han, Grass Roots Restaurant, Alexandria, Va., U.S.A.; Carol Gvozdich, Alexandria, Va., U.S.A.; Kathy Hardesty, Colombia, Md., U.S.A.; Nancy Lendved, Alexandria, Va., U.S.A.; Ken Pierpoint, Owings Mills, Md., U.S.A.; Ann Ready, Alexandria, Va., U.S.A; Tajuana Queen, Washington, D.C.; Linda Robertson, Jud Tile, Vienna, Va., U.S.A.; Troiano Marble, Beltsville, Md., U.S.A.; Tina Ujlaki, New York, N.Y.; Phyllis Van Auken Antiques, Kensington, Md., U.S.A.; Rita Walters, London; Sarah Wiley, London.; CiCi Williamson, Alexandria, Va., U.S.A.

The editors also thank the following: The American Hand Plus, Washington, D.C.; Moira Banks, London;

Stuart Berman, Washington, D.C.; Dr. John Brown, Health Education Council, London; Max Busetti, National Pasta Association, Arlington, Va., U.S.A.; Jackie Chalkley, Washington, D.C.; China Closet, Bethesda, Md., U.S.A.; Nic Colling, Home Produce Company, Alexandria, Va., U.S.A.; Lynn Corbyn, Burgess Hill, Sussex, England; Shirley Corriher, Atlanta, Ga., U.S.A.; Sonny Di Martino, Safeway, Alexandria, Va., U.S.A.; Rex Downey, Oxon Hill, Md., U.S.A.; Dennis Drake, Dr. Jacob Exler, Ruth Matthews, U.S. Department of Agriculture, Hyattsville, Md., U.S.A.; Flowers Unique, Inc., Alexandria, Va., U.S.A.; Susan Gatenby, King's College London (Kensington Campus), London; Kitchen Bazaar, Washington, D.C.; Kossow Gourmet Produce, Washington, D.C.; A. Litteri, Inc.,

Washington, D.C.; Marie Lou, Golden Wok Restaurant, Washington, D.C.; Nick Lyddane, Imperial Produce, Washington, D.C.; Ron Naman, Sutton Place Gourmet, Washington, D.C.; E. and R. Nevy, Cumberland Macaroni Manufacturing Co., Cumberland, Md., U.S.A.; Lisa Ownby, Alexandria, Va., U.S.A.; The Pasta Information Centre, London; Leon Pinto, Gourmand, Inc., Alexandria, Va., U.S.A.; Joyce Piotrowski, Vienna, Va., U.S.A.; Jerry Purdy, Giant Food, Landover, Md., U.S.A.; Tin T. Quang, East Wind Restaurant, Alexandria, Va., U.S.A.; J. Rzepny, Ticonderoga Farms, Chantilly, Va., U.S.A.; Ronnie Sarragaso, Sutton Place Gourmet, Bethesda, Md., U.S.A.; Straight from the Crate, Inc., Alexandria, Va., U.S.A.; U.S. Fish, Alexandria, Va., and Kensington, Md., U.S.A.; Williams-Sonoma, Washington, D.C.

Typesetting by G. Beard & Sons Ltd., Brighton, Sussex, England.
Printed and bound by Oriental Press, Dubai.